*Crossway Bible Guides*

Series editors: Ian Coffey (NT), Stephen Gaukroger (OT)
Old Testament editor: Stephen Dray

**Also in this series:**

# *Psalms 73–150: Crossway Bible Guide*

## Alan Palmer and Debra Reid

Crossway Books Leicester

CROSSWAY BOOKS
*38 De Montfort Street, Leicester LE1 7GP, England*

First published 1998

**British Library Cataloguing in Publication Data**
A catalogue record for this book is available from the British Library.

ISBN 1–85684–179–0

Set in Palatino

Typeset in Great Britain by Textype Typesetters, Cambridge
Printed in Great Britain

For my wife and best friend, Pennie,
and my children
Sam and Alex

(*Alan Palmer*)


For
my husband David,
and our friends Neil and Angie Robinson
and Simon and Linda Smith
with thanks for your daily
practical support

(*Debra Reid*)

# CONTENTS

# Welcome!

These days, meeting together to study the Bible in groups appears to be a booming leisure-time activity in many parts of the world. In the United Kingdom alone, it is estimated that over one million people each week meet in home Bible-study groups.

This series has been designed to help such groups and, in particular, those who lead them. These Bible guides are also very suitable for individual study, and may help hard-pressed preachers, teachers and students too (see *How to use this Bible Guide*).

We have therefore enlisted authors who are in the business of teaching the Bible to others and are doing it well. They have kept in their sights two clear aims:

1. To explain and apply the message of the Bible in non-technical language.
2. To encourage discussion, prayer and action on what the Bible teaches.

All of us engaged in the project believe that the Bible is the Word of God – given to us in order that people might discover him and his purposes for our lives. We believe that the sixty-six books which go to make up the Bible, although written by different people, in different places, at different times, through different circumstances, have a single unifying theme: that theme is Salvation. This means free forgiveness and the removal of all our guilt, it means the gift of eternal life, and it means the wholeness of purpose and joy which God has designed us to experience here and now, all of this being made possible through the Lord Jesus Christ.

# How to use this Bible Guide

These guides have been prepared both for personal study and for the leaders and members of small groups. More information about group study follows on the next few pages.

You can use this book very profitably as a personal study guide. The short studies are ideal for daily reading: the first of the questions provided is usually aimed to help you with personal reflection (see *How to tackle personal Bible study*). If you prefer to settle down to a longer period of study, you can use groups of three to five studies, and thus get a better overview of a longer Bible passage. In either case, using the Bible Guide will help you to be disciplined about regular study, a habit that countless Christians have found greatly beneficial. (See also *How to tackle Psalms 73–150* for methods of selecting studies if you do not intend to use them all.)

Yet a third use for these Bible Guides is as a quarry for ideas for the busy Bible teacher, providing outlines and application for those giving talks or sermons or teaching children. You will need more than this book can offer of course, but the way the Bible text is broken down, comments offered and questions raised may well suggest directions to follow.

## How to tackle personal Bible study

We have already suggested that you might use this book as a personal study guide. Now for some more detail.

One of the best methods of Bible study is to read the text through carefully several times, possibly using different versions or translations. Having reflected on the material, it is a good discipline to write down your own thoughts before doing anything else. At this stage it can be useful to consult another background book. See *Resources* on page 15 and *Further reading* on page 216. If you are using this book as your main study resource, then read through the relevant sections carefully, turning up the Bible references that are mentioned. The questions at the end of each chapter are specifically designed to help you to apply the passage to your own situation. You may find it helpful to write your answers to the questions in your notes.

It is a good habit to conclude with prayer, bringing before God the things you have learned.

If this kind of in-depth study is too demanding for you and you have only a short time at your disposal, read the Bible passage, read the comments in the Bible Guide, think round one of the questions and commit what you have learned to God in a brief prayer. This would take about fifteen minutes without rushing it.

## How to tackle your group Bible study

### 1. Getting help

If you are new to leading groups, you will obviously want to get all the help you can from ministers and experienced friends. Books are also extremely helpful and we strongly recommend a book prepared by the editors of this series of Bible Guides: *Housegroups: the leaders' survival guide*, edited by Ian Coffey and Stephen Gaukroger (Crossway Books, 1996). This book looks at the whole range of different types of group, asking what is the point of it all, what makes a good leader, how to tackle your meeting, how to help the members, how to study, pray, share, worship and plenty of other pointers, tips and guidelines.

This book is a 'must' for all leaders of small groups. It is written by a team of people widely experienced in this area. It is available at your local Christian bookshop. If you have difficulty in obtaining a copy write to Crossway Books, Norton Street, Nottingham, NG7 3HR, UK.

### 2. Planning a programme with your Bible Guide

This guide is a commentary on God's Word, written to help a group to get the most out of their studies. Although it is never ideal to chop up Scripture into small pieces, which the authors never intended, huge chunks are indigestible and we have tried to provide a diet of bite-sized mouthfuls.

If you want to get an overview of the Bible book in a series of meetings, you will need to select appropriate studies for each meeting. Read them yourself first and prepare a short summary of the studies you are tackling for your group. Ideally you could write it on a sheet of A5 paper and hand a copy to each member.

Do not attempt to pack more than one study into one meeting but choose the crucial one, the study which best crystallizes the message. There are examples in *How to tackle Psalms 73–150* below.

If you do not intend to cover the whole Bible book, choose a series of studies to suit the number of meetings you have available. It is a good idea to use consecutive studies, not to dodge about. You will then build up a detailed picture of one section of Scripture. Alternative examples of programmes of study for this book are given in *How to tackle Psalms 73–150*.

## 3. Resources

You will find any or all of these books of great value in providing background to your Bible knowledge. Put some of them on your Christmas list and build up your library.

*New Bible Dictionary* or *New Concise Bible Dictionary* (IVP)
*New Bible Atlas* (IVP)
*New Bible Commentary (21st Century edition)* (IVP)
*Handbook of Life in Bible Times* John Thompson (IVP)
*The Bible User's Manual* (IVP)
*The Lion Handbook to the Bible* (Lion Publishing)
*The Message of the Bible* (Lion Publishing)
*NIV Study Bible* (Hodder & Stoughton)
*The Bible with Pleasure* Stephen Motyer (Crossways Books)

The relevant volume in the IVP Tyndale Commentary series will give you reliable and detailed help with any knotty points you may encounter.

## 4. Preparing to lead

Reading, discussing with friends, studying, praying, reflecting on life . . . preparation can be endless. But do not be daunted by that. If you wait to become the perfect leader you will never start at all. The really vital elements in preparation are:

▶ prayer (not only in words but an attitude of dependence on God: 'Lord, I can't manage this on my own')

▶ familiarity with the study passage (careful reading of the text, the Bible Guide study and any other resource books that throw light on it) and

▶ a clear idea of where you hope to get in the meeting (notes on your introduction, perhaps, recap what was covered at the last meeting, and what direction you hope the questions will take you in – don't force the group to give your answers).

Here is a short checklist for the busy group leader:

Have I prayed about the meeting?

Have I decided exactly what I want to achieve through the meeting?

Have I prepared the material?

Am I clear about the questions that will encourage positive group discussion?

Am I gently encouraging silent members?

Am I, again gently, quietening the chatterers?

Am I willing to admit ignorance?

Am I willing to listen to what the group says and to value their contributions?

Am I ready not to be dogmatic, not imposing my ideas on the group?

Have I planned how to involve the group in discovering for themselves?

Have I developed several 'prayer points' that will help focus the group?

Are we applying Scripture to our experience of real life or only using it as a peg to hang our opinions on?

Are we finding resources for action and change or just having a nice talk?

Are we all enjoying the experience together?

## How to tackle Psalms 73–150

Now let's assume that you are planning an eight-week course of studies (you will have to make adjustments if you have more or fewer meetings). Where do you begin? This is entirely up to you and your groups of course, but to get you started, here are some possible routes you might take.

### 1. 'Top selection'

Some psalms are justly famous, and if you have to miss out on the majority why not go for the best known and loved ones? Such as: Psalms 95, 96, 100, 104, 121, 137, 145 and 150.

### 2. Study a collection

In his introduction to Psalms in the *New Bible Commentary 21st Century edition*, J. A. Motyer suggests that the book of Psalms includes a number of smaller collections. He has suggested titles for some of them:

'Jerusalem Praise', 93–100. For an eight-week course.
'Pilgrim Praise', 120–136. For a course of studies, choose any eight (or however many you need).
'A Salvation Cantata', 113–118. A short five-study course.
'The Endless Hallelujah', 111–113 and 146–150. Five studies on eight psalms.
Psalms of Asaph, 73–83. Take your pick.

### 3. Pursue a theme

Choose a theme such as problems and solutions: human experience and God's provision, e.g. Psalms 73, 74, 88, 109, 121, 129, 137, 142.

Or use the contents list on pp. 7–11 to pick out psalms on the theme of God's glory, joy, peace, and so on.

### 4. Selected themes

Pick psalms to represent a cross-section of the various themes that are significant in the book of Psalms, e.g.:

Psalm 100 Praise and thankfulness

Psalms 130–131 Forgiveness and peace
Psalm 99 Worship and God's holiness
Psalm 119:1–16 God's Word
Psalm 91 Security in God
Psalm 93 God's rule
Psalm 77 Feeling far from God
Psalm 85 Restoration

These outlines are meant to be springboards for your own ideas, so please do not follow them slavishly. Adapt them for your own use, merge them or ignore them. In any case many of the psalms will have to be left out of your studies, so why not begin or end your meeting by reading one or two psalms as an aid to worship? This will give you a better flavour of the whole book of Psalms and, remember, the psalms were meant to be sung, danced or wept as well as studied.

## What can we expect to learn from the Psalms?

*All Scripture is God-breathed and is useful* (2 Timothy 3:16). So how can the Psalms be 'useful' to us in our fellowship today?

The Psalms bring us into the nearer presence of God by:

▶ Showing us that our worship can legitimately include elements of the arts, i.e. music, poetry, drama and dance.

▶ Acting as a 'mirror for our souls', i.e. showing us what we are really like, both as a church or fellowship and as individuals.

▶ Giving us words to express to God how we feel about him, his work and his creation. Also the Psalms help us more fully to express how we feel about everything that impacts on our lives. They give us words of praise and, when we need it, words to seek God's pardon.

▶ Corporately and personally, they can be used to renew our energy and resolve to live the life of faith.

# Finding your way round this book

**In our Bible Guides we have developed special symbols to make things easier to follow. Every study therefore has an opening section which is the passage in a nutshell.**

 The main section is the one that *makes sense of the passage*.

### Questions

Every passage also has special questions for personal and group study after the main section. Some questions are addressed to us as individuals, some speak to us as members of our church or home group, while others concern us as members of God's people worldwide. The questions are deliberately designed:

▶ to get people thinking about the passage

▶ to apply the text to 'real life' situations

▶ to encourage reflection, discussion and action!

As a group leader you may well discover additional questions that will have special relevance to your group, so look out for these and note them in your preparation time.

## Digging deeper

Some passages, however, require an extra amount of explanation, and we have put these sections into two categories. The first kind gives additional background material that helps us to understand something complex. For example, if we dig deeper into the gospels, it helps us to know who the Pharisees were, so that we can see more easily why they related to Jesus in the way they did. These technical sections are marked with a spade.

## Important doctrines

The second kind of background section appears with passages which have important doctrines contained in them and which we need to study in more depth if we are to grow as Christians. Special sections that explain them to us in greater detail are marked with a face as above.

# Welcome to the Psalms

## Rave reviews!

Down the centuries the Psalms have fired the minds and imaginations of many Christians. Ambrose of Milan considered the Psalms the height of spirituality, viewing them as 'a kind of medicine for the salvation of the soul'. The German reformer Martin Luther thought them so important that he produced a 'New Testament and Psalms' version of the Bible, a practice followed by some publishers even today.

In the last century the great Baptist preacher C. H. Spurgeon spent over twenty years studying the Psalms. The result was his massive commentary, *The Treasury of David*. On completion of this monumental task he declared that he would never find a 'richer store house'.

In our own day enthusiasm for the Psalms has not diminished. Dr Billy Graham is so convinced about their benefits that he encourages all his listeners to read the Psalms regularly. He suggests that people follow his own practice of reading five psalms a day. In this way they can get through the entire collection in a month.

For many churches around the world the Psalms, either sung or read, are a vital aspect of their corporate worship. In a few churches they are the only musical contribution.

## Why are the Psalms so popular?

Why are so many people attracted to the Psalms and what makes them so readable? There are three main reasons that contribute to their enduring popularity.

## The Psalms reveal a God who has a heart for the arts

The Psalms are alive and attractive because they are so full of music. The title of the book of Psalms in the Greek version of the Old Testament (the Septuagint) is *psalmoi*. This originally indicated 'a striking or twitching of the fingers on a string'. It came to mean 'a sacred song accompanied by instruments'. The Psalms were written primarily to be sung, not read. Ronald Allen says that 'One can more easily separate dance from the dancer than Psalms from music. In music Psalms come alive.'

There are many references to the use of instruments in the Psalms (e.g. Psalm 150). There are also musical instructions to be found in many of the titles (e.g. Psalm 22). While we do not know what all these instructions mean, this should not prevent us from putting our own music to these ancient songs. It would be wrong to miss the significance of the fact that the longest book in the Bible is a book of music. Martin Luther wrote, 'He who despises music does not please me. Music is a gift of God, not a gift of men. After theology I accord to music the highest place and the highest honour.'

The title of the book of Psalms in the Hebrew Bible is *tehillim*. This simply means 'Praises'. Robert Weber writes, 'Here is the heart of praise for the Old Testament people of God.' If this is the case, then 'music' must be considered as a vital ingredient of praise and worship. It seems that, when the Holy Spirit is at work among the people of God, it is not long before there is a new song on their lips (Ephesians 5:18–20).

## The Psalms reveal a God with a passion for poetry

One quarter of the Old Testament is in poetic form. The Psalms are simply poetry set to music. The most reasonable explanation for this is that poetry is the best medium with which to communicate our feelings. For, as Laurence Perrine writes, poetry is 'a kind of language that says more and says it more intensively than does ordinary language'. Here we find words to express to God how we really feel.

When we call the Psalms 'poetry' we should be aware that Hebrew poetry is quite different from the rhyming variety that we may be familiar with. Professor Alan Harmon reminds us that the book of Psalms has to 'be read as a Middle Eastern Book of poetry translated into English'.

Its poetic form is based around a literary structure known as 'parallelism'. This is where the same idea is described in different ways to give a fuller sense of meaning. There are various different types of parallelism to be found in the Psalms.

Sometimes the first line of a pair is echoed in the second.

> O LORD, how many are my foes!
> How many rise up against me!
>
> (Psalm 3:1)

Sometimes the second line develops the first line a bit further, often adding ideas or elements to the original thought:

> Come, let us bow down in worship,
> let us kneel before the LORD our Maker.
>
> (Psalm 95:6)

In some cases the second line begins with 'but', and presents the opposite of the first line:

> For evil men will be cut off,
> but those who hope in the LORD will inherit the land.
>
> (Psalm 37:9)

In other cases the first line is explained by the second, often with figures of speech or word pictures:

> Your tongue plots destruction;
> it is like a sharpened razor,
> you who practise deceit.
>
> (Psalm 52:2)

Students of the Psalms believe that it is possible to divide them up into different 'categories' or 'types'. Whether a particular psalm fits in these categories is determined by content and literary structure. While it is not possible for every psalm to be categorized in this way, certain 'types' of psalms are recognizable.

Five of the main types of psalms are:

▶ a hymn of praise (e.g. Psalms 8, 19, 33, 103, 145–150)

▶ a song of thanksgiving (e.g. Psalms 18, 21, 92, 138)

▶ a lament by an individual or community (e.g. Psalms 3, 5, 13, 17, 22, 31, 44, 80, 126, 137)

▶ a song of trust and meditation (e.g. Psalms 11, 16, 23, 91, 121, 131)

▶ a wisdom psalm (e.g. Psalms 37, 49, 73, 112, 128, 133).

## The Psalms reveal a God who has provided psalms for all seasons

In the middle of the Bible God has provided what Saint Augustine called 'a looking glass of the soul'. Here we can see ourselves and our situations. There is nothing we can experience which is not reflected in the writings of the psalmist. John Calvin recognized this when he called the book of Psalms the 'anatomy of the soul'. He went on to say that 'there is not an emotion of which anyone can be conscious that is not here represented as in a mirror'.

The Psalms not only reflect what is going on in our lives, they also give us the words to express to God how we feel about it. Saint Athanasius wrote, 'Most of Scripture speaks to us while the Psalms speak for us.' Here we can find appropriate words to tell the Lord exactly what is going on in our lives. The Psalms are not only songs for us to sing, they can also become prayers that we can pray.

## Who wrote the Psalms?

We know that King David was a gifted composer and musician (see 2 Samuel 23:1). It is hardly surprising then to find that nearly half of the songs in the book of Psalms are attributed to him, seventy-three in all. But he is not the only author who contributed to this marvellous collection.

Familiar characters like King Solomon (Psalms 72 and 127) and Moses (Psalm 90) make their contribution. Other writers may be less well known to us. A man named Asaph has twelve psalms attributed to him (Psalms 50, 73–83). Two psalms are by Heman and Ethan, the Ezrahites (Psalms 88 and 89). A further twelve psalms are written by a family group known as 'the sons of Korah' (Psalms 42–49, 84–85 and 87–88). There are also 'anonymous psalms' whose writers remain unknown to us (Psalms 1, 2, 33, 66, 111–121 *etc.*). However, because David wrote the majority of the psalms, the collection is most often linked to his name. That is why we refer to them as 'The Psalms of David'.

## When were the Psalms written?

Half the psalms were written by David in the tenth century BC. Some were written much earlier than this and some much later. Psalm 90 is the earliest we can date and it comes from Moses in the fifteenth century BC. One of the latest, Psalm 137, was written by a Jewish exile who had returned to Jerusalem from Babylon in the late fifth century BC. This means that the Psalms we have today were written over a thousand-year period.

## How are the Psalms put together?

The Psalter (the technical name for the collection of psalms) contains five Books of Psalms. It is modelled on the 'Pentateuch' (the five books of Moses, i.e. Genesis to Deuteronomy). Orthodox Jewish teaching is that Moses gave Israel the five books of the Law. King David's gift was the five books of poetry, known as the Psalms. The books are as follows:

> Book 1  Psalms 1–41
> Book 2  Psalms 42–72
> Book 3  Psalms 73–89
> Book 4  Psalms 90–106
> Book 5  Psalms 107–150

## Titles and technical terms

The titles or superscriptions which we find at the top of many of the psalms were probably added a long time after the original song was written. Possibly these additions were made by an editor when the psalms were being put together into a collection. They usually either contain some musical instruction or give some historical background to the psalm. Some psalms have no titles.

## Cursing psalms

There are a number of psalms which contain a strong element of seeming vindictiveness, hatred or cursing. These have caused real problems to Christians and non-Christians alike. The best way to deal with these psalms, especially in the light of the New Testament, is not to ignore them but to seek to understand and face their concerns squarely. Here are some of the factors to consider:

1. They have been included in the Bible. This means that we must take them seriously (see 2 Timothy 3:16).
2. They are spoken in the context of faith, believing God alone should execute vengeance.
3. The psalmist thinks of his enemies as God's enemies, who, as such, are to be hated.
4. David was in no way a vindictive man.
5. The New Testament actually emphasizes the reality of judgment on all evil doers.
6. Christians may not wish to take and use these cries for themselves but may prefer to 'translate them into affirmations of God's judgment and into denunciations of the "spiritual hosts of wickedness" which are the real enemy' (Derek Kidner, *Psalms 1–73*, IVP, 1973, p 32).

Above all, we need to remind ourselves that the Psalms are 'the windows of the soul'. They are an honest expression of what the psalmist was really thinking at the time. The truth is that none of us have been completely free of such thoughts. This is probably why we find these 'cursing psalms' so uncomfortable to read. The psalmists' total openness can be very threatening indeed! It is comforting to know that J. I. Packer's words remain true for all of us: 'God knows the absolute worst about us and yet still loves us.'

Examples of cursing psalms include: Psalms 7, 35, 58, 59, 69, 109, 137, 139. Some psalms contain a smaller element: Psalms 5:10; 17:13; 40:14; 55:9; 104:35; 129:5.

## How did the ancient people of God use the Psalms?

Although they were written by individuals, the Psalms came to play a vital role in the spiritual life of the whole community of Israel. They were 'Israel's hymnbook' and were used extensively in the context of corporate worship.

Psalms were sung by pilgrims as they made their way up to Jerusalem to worship at the temple. These are known as the 'songs of ascents' (Psalms 120–134). The temple choirs used them as dramatic 'sung requests' to gain entry to the place of worship (Psalm 24). The congregation used them to express their worship to God for his greatness, forgiveness, love and mercy (Psalms 8, 22, 48, 51, 65, 103). When it came to a time of praise, the Psalms were much in evidence (Psalms 145–150). The Psalms were very much part of the very fabric of Jewish worship. They still are today.

## How are the Psalms used in the New Testament?

When we turn to the New Testament we discover that the Psalms figure significantly. The Lord Jesus himself sang the Psalms all his life. When he came to Jerusalem with his parents for the Feast of Passover he would have sung the songs of ascents (Psalms 120–134). In celebrating the Passover each year, he would have sung the Hallel Psalms (Psalms 113–118, 136 cf. p. 140).

Those who wrote the history of his life saw in the Psalms references to him. For instance:

- When Jesus entered Jerusalem, the crowds greeted him with words taken directly from the Psalms (Luke 19:38 and Psalm 118:26).

- In his debates with the authorities, Jesus referred to their rejection of him by appealing to the Psalms (Luke 20:17–18 and Psalm 118:22).

- In a discussion of who he really was, again Jesus pointed people back to the Psalms (Luke 20:42–43 and Psalm 110:1).

▶ The Lord Jesus took part in singing some of the Psalms at the Last Supper (Matthew 26:30).

▶ When he was facing the most awful suffering on the cross, he cried out using words taken from Israel's ancient hymn book (Matthew 27:46; Mark 15:34 and Psalm 22:1).

▶ The words of the priests who threw abuse at him, while he hung on the cross, seem to be echoes of sentiments expressed in the Psalms (Matthew 27:39–44; Mark 15:31–32; Luke 23:35 and Psalm 22:7–8).

▶ The fact that the soldiers left his garment undivided was seen as a fulfilment of what was written by the psalmist (John 19:23–24 and Psalm 22:18).

▶ The gruesome physical effects of crucifixion are apparently predicted in Psalm 22:14–17.

▶ Even the Lord Jesus' last words on the cross, 'into your hands I commit my spirit', were taken directly from Psalm 31:5 (Luke 23:46).

Following the resurrection, Jesus managed to convince two discouraged disciples that he was the Messiah by referring back to the Old Testament Scriptures. He showed them how all these writings were pointing forward to him and his mission and ministry. There is little doubt that the Psalms were a part of this Bible study that Jesus conducted. This guided tour of the Old Testament led to these two disciples experiencing a new revelation of Christ and what someone has called 'spiritual heartburn' (Luke 24:32). Later Jesus told all the gathered disciples that the Psalms were a major part of his teaching programme while he was with them (Luke 24:44). It is no wonder that all the early writers of the New Testament felt that the Psalms were so important in their understanding of who Jesus was and what he had come to do.

Ronald Allen says that the New Testament is 'awash with the Psalms'. There are approximately 360 quotations from the Hebrew Bible in the New Testament and nearly one-third (112) of these are from the Psalms.

The early Christians turned to the Psalms and saw Jesus pictured there. They also turned to the Psalms to find texts to preach on concerning the resurrection (Acts 2:25–28, 34–35; Psalms 16:8–11; 110:1). In times of testing and persecution they looked for comfort and encouragement there as well (Acts 4:23–26 and Psalm 2:1–2).

## How should we read the Psalms for ourselves?

As we read these wonderful songs we can learn more about what pleases God. We can identify with the experiences of those who wrote them. We can grow in our devotion to the Lord. If we have been flagging spiritually we may even find that they give us a new enthusiasm for the life of Faith. The words of Saint Augustine are a fitting summary. He said that the Psalms 'kindled his love for God, (and) they breathed fresh life into his spiritual pilgrimage'.

# BOOK 3 (Psalms 73–89)

## Asaph the psalmist

Book 3 of the collection of songs called 'the Psalms' begins with Psalm 73. Its title or 'superscription' tells us that its author is Asaph, and it is the first of eleven psalms of Asaph (Psalms 73–83).

To begin with, we need to notice two important things about Asaph.

*His career.* Asaph was a leader in ancient Israel and familiar with sacred things. His own brothers elected him as a chief singer in the temple (1 Chronicles 15:16–17). King David appointed him the chief minister in the temple (1 Chronicles 16:4–5). He was also a founder of one of the temple choirs, and a kind of director of music (1 Chronicles 25:1–2).

Socially and spiritually, Asaph appeared to be well established, but appearances can be deceptive. In Psalm 73:2 he admits that, at one time, he almost walked away from God. He nearly made a 'shipwreck' of his faith.

*His candour.* What you notice about Asaph is that he is very honest about his personal struggle. He is open about his battles with belief. We can learn a simple lesson from this ancient song writer: being honest about our doubts, instead of covering them up, is spiritually liberating. The Russian writer Dostoevsky once wrote that, 'It is not as a child that I believe and confess Christ. My hosanna is born of a furnace of doubt.'

Asaph had come very close to 'throwing in the towel' from a spiritual point of view. However, he begins Psalm 73 with a strong statement of his own belief (verse 1). How was this possible in view of his doubts? This statement was written after his time of testing; he is looking back on the dark valley of doubt that he has just been through. Now he has a renewed sense of confidence, and he has grown through this difficult experience (see 1 Peter 1:6–7 and James 1:2–4).

# Psalm 73

## 'The lucky wicked'

**Why do good things happen to bad people?**

Asaph reflects on the tortuous pilgrimage that had brought him to the new found confidence in God that he expresses in verse 1. He recounts in verse 2 that 'his feet had  almost slipped'. Why was this so? One reason was that he had 'envied the arrogant' (verse 3). It seemed to Asaph that those who ignored God had a lot going for them. They were, in his opinion, 'the lucky wicked'. We often ask, 'Why do bad things happen to good people?' Asaph is asking, 'Why do good things happen to bad people?' It isn't fair!

To Asaph, these wicked people appeared to be materially wealthy (verses 3, 12). They seemed to have excessive amounts of disposable income, while Asaph had little or none. As Christians, it's not too hard to put ourselves in Asaph's place. There have been times in all our lives when we have been envious of those who appear to have more of this world's goods than we do. The people who Asaph envied were not only materially wealthy, they were also physically healthy (verses 4–5). They appeared to him to be 'healthy and strong' and 'free from the burdens common to man'. They even seemed to die peacefully in their sleep, as they did not have struggles at their death (see NIV footnote on the Hebrew text of these verses). All this seemed true for the wicked, while Asaph was dogged by suffering and bouts of ill health (verse 14). This is not as it should be.

Asaph thinks that God owes him something. He has been living a pure, fully committed life and so he feels that he should be wealthy and healthy. However, Christians are not guaranteed a life of ease and health. There are times when we are brought low by financial reversals or illness, and it is in these times that we learn the truth of Paul's words in 2 Corinthians 12:9: God's grace is sufficient for us.

These people were wealthy and healthy and also popular socially (verses 6–9, 10–11). The people 'praise them' (verse 10, RSV). Society could find no fault with them and they literally 'drink up' the popular praise. These people were so arrogant that they believed that even God was not in a position to interfere in their high-flying lives (verse 11). Asaph was not popular; he did not enter rooms to rapturous applause. He was honest, yes; but an honest nobody. As a result he was both envious and discontented with his situation. This led him to begin to doubt God. His spiritual foundations began to shake. He almost 'lost it' spiritually. Almost, but not quite. He made a remarkable spiritual recovery.

In verses 13–15 there is a distinct change of direction. Notice how many times the personal pronoun 'I' is used. It slowly dawns on Asaph how selfish his attitude is. He acknowledges how self-centred he had been; his prayers have been focused exclusively on himself and his wants. He begins to consider other believers as well as himself (verse 15). He realizes that public declarations of personal doubt are not always appropriate.

In verses 16–20 he describes how he entered the sanctuary of God. As he began to worship he began to see things more clearly. In worship we lift our thoughts and feelings to God. We tend to be raised above our problems and begin to see them from God's perspective. Asaph sees the people he envied as they really were (verse 17). They were not sound and secure, they were set on 'slippery ground'. They were not always going to be wealthy; they would eventually face both financial and spiritual 'ruin' (verse 18), ending their lives not peacefully, but in terror (verse 19). To God these people's future was like a dream that disappears as one wakes up (verse 20). The wicked are not to be envied by the believer but pitied. As Asaph worshipped, he was gripped by the perspective of eternity, he viewed others differently and received forgiveness for himself. There is little doubt that, while Asaph was in the sanctuary, he heard the word of God. Part of worship is to listen to God's word and to respond to it (see Malachi 2:7).

Asaph admits that he could see no way through his dilemma until he entered the sanctuary and met with the living God (verses 21–22). He recognizes that up until that point he had been reacting instinctively, more like 'a brute beast' than a believer made in the image of God (compare these verses with Psalm 32:9).

Asaph now glories in God's sufficiency (verses 23–26). He recognizes that God is with him even in the dark times of doubt. He discovers that God not only keeps him safe but leads him in the right paths (verse 24, see also Psalms 23:3 and 119:105). This divine direction will eventually lead the psalmist right to heaven's door (verse 24, see also Philippians 1:6 and Jude 24).

In verses 25–26 we can see that confidence has now replaced lack of confidence. Even when he faces death, Asaph believes that this will not be the end, but the beginning of eternity with God. Asaph resolves to tell others that he has put his complete confidence in God (verses 27–28). This is a sure sign of spiritual renewal. Those filled with the Spirit of God want to proclaim the good news of God to all around them. Now Asaph does not envy the wicked, he grieves for them. For him wealth and popularity do not count in the end; living close to God is ultimately the most vital thing in life.

## Questions

1. Have you ever been in a situation where it appeared that someone was benefiting from bad behaviour? How did it feel? Why?
2. How can the local church help Christians to regain the right

perspective of 'God' and 'life' through worship?

3. How can Christians show to society that it is relationships that really matter, not things?

# Psalm 74

## Smashed to pieces by God?

---

**A mystery: are we the object of God's anger?**

---

We have already seen that Asaph has had his struggles with 'Why do good things happen to bad people?' in Psalm 73; now in Psalm 74 he explores the reasons for 'Why do bad things happen to good people?'

The title tells us that this psalm is a *maskil*. This Hebrew word, which occurs thirteen times in the Psalms, can be translated 'to make wise' or 'prudent'. Perhaps these songs were written in order that Israel might learn the lessons of history. This particular psalm certainly has some harsh lessons to teach.

It appears that Asaph was writing a song not only that he could sing but also that could provide words for the whole nation in a time of national defeat, destruction and sadness. Both the writer and the nation feel that they have been rejected by God and that he is venting his anger on them (verse 1). The psalmist reminds the Lord of the 'good old days' when he redeemed his people, who were considered to be a valuable inheritance. Asaph also speaks about 'Mount Zion' (another name for Jerusalem), where God's people were able to experience his presence (verse 2).

The psalmist reviews the recent past. It appears that he is describing the 'sacking' of Jerusalem by a fearsome enemy. The city is now nothing more than a pile of bricks. The temple itself seems to have been attacked and destroyed (verse 3). Asaph may be referring to the Babylonian destruction of Jerusalem in 587 BC (see also Zechariah 7:1–6; 8:18–19; and the book of Lamentations). These ancient 'storm troopers' were ruthlessly effective. Now, where the psalmist and others used to meet the Lord, they meet only the contempt of their conquerors. The ruthless invaders apparently stripped off all the gold inlay from the temple before burning the wooden structure. They desecrated the holy place, placed their battle-colours there and sought to destroy everywhere that people might go to seek God (verses 3–8).

In the light of this terrible destruction, Asaph and the people felt abandoned by God. There were no signs of his presence, mercy or care. There was no comforting word from the Lord for them to hang on to, and no-one was sure just how long this terrible state of affairs would last (verse 9). Asaph wants to know how long God is going to put up with this state of affairs. How long will he tolerate this blatant ridiculing of both his name and his nature (verse 10)? Why does he seem to be holding back from avenging himself? It is not as if God lacks the power to act.

The psalmist is just one of many who have felt the pain of going through a time in their lives when God seems to be both silent and inactive. It is difficult to continue believing in a God who is both powerful and good when you are experiencing neither of these divine qualities in your own situation. When you so obviously need God's help, why does he appear to refrain from giving it (verse 11)?

## New confidence

Something seems to have happened between verses 11 and 12, however. The psalmist's situation has not improved but he seems to have a new sense of confidence in God. Now Asaph rehearses a glorious past. In going over what God has done in the past, the psalmist gains new strength to believe that he will act in the present and the future. For the writer recalls that God is a great King, that God is the supreme Saviour of his people, and that he is the mighty Creator of all that exists (verses 12–17).

With all this positive information at hand, Asaph goes on to remind God of what the enemies of Israel are doing, how they are treating his people with contempt (verse 18). Asaph prays that the Lord will not allow his 'dove', i.e. his chosen people, to be devoured by wild beasts (verse 19). The term 'dove' is 'a term of tender affection' (see Song of Songs 6:9). The psalmist believes that God is a God who keeps his promises (i.e. the covenant). The 'oppressed' must not be allowed to suffer 'disgrace'. It is time for God to rise up and deal with these aggressors.

A former minister of Westminster Chapel, London, says regarding Psalm 74: 'When the heart is hot and restless, and it seems as though God has forsaken his own, he is a wise person who turns to Him in song, even though the song be only a complaint' (G. Campbell Morgan, *Notes on the Psalms*, Henry E. Walter, 1946, p. 62). There is nothing unspiritual in telling God exactly how you feel about your circumstances. This kind of 'pressure release' to the Lord may well act as a spiritual valve and prevent an emotional explosion.

## Questions

1. What really makes you angry, and why?
2. What is to be the attitude of Christians toward those who try to destroy the church? Reflect upon Acts 4:23–31.
3. Why will it be the church rather than the world that will triumph in the end? What do we mean by 'triumph'?

# Psalm 75

## God is on our side

**God intervenes in personal and national history.**

The title for this psalm gives us some interesting details. To begin with, it is addressed to the 'director of music', i.e. the choir director. From this we can ascertain that Asaph intended this song to be sung by the gathered community of God in a time of worship. The tune for this song is called 'Do not destroy', and was possibly a popular ditty of the day connected with the grape harvest (see Isaiah 65:8). The double use of 'A psalm' and 'A song' indicates that this is a formal poem by Asaph which, because of its popularity, had become virtually an institution.

Basically Psalm 75 answers the desperate request made by Asaph in Psalm 74:22. God had seemed so far away in the previous psalm, but now Asaph can say, 'Your Name is near' (verse 1). The mention of 'Name' indicates 'all that God has revealed himself to be'. God's Name is part of his self-revelation to his people (see Exodus 3:4–14; 34:5ff., 14). A further meaning of 'your Name is near' is that here is an opportunity to turn to him in prayer (see Acts 2:21). The fact that people are telling of God's wonderful deeds suggests that they were strengthening their faith by this process. It was a case of 'Count your blessings, name them one by one, and it will surprise you what the Lord has done.'

Asaph recognizes that God decides when it is the right time to act. When he acts you can be sure that he will always do the right thing (verse 2). Sometimes it seems that God waits until the very foundations of our lives totter. He will not act until that point because he knows too well that, if he does, we will imagine that we can save ourselves (verses 2–7; see also 2 Corinthians 1:9). (Note: Derek Kidner writes that 'the appointed time' in verse 2 is actually an important concept in the Old Testament account of God's ordering of the world. It is used for 'the "seasons" of the year, with their steady rhythm [Genesis 1:14]' and for 'the "appointment of feasts" [Leviticus 23:2] which gave the annual pattern of worship' [Kidner, p. 271].)

The imagery in verse 7 is that of a subject seeking mercy from a king. The person seeking favour lies flat on his face in front of the monarch. He waits for the decision which will result in his life being taken or spared. If the king reaches down his hand and lifts the supplicant's head, it means his life is to be spared. It is God who will lift up the head of one to receive mercy, and pour out his cup of wrath on another in judgment. In the final analysis, it is God's right to judge. This paints a picture of God who is above all. There is no-one bigger than he. The enemies of Israel and our spiritual enemies pale into insignificance beside him (verse 8). (Note that the term 'cup' in verse 8 is often linked with God's judgments [see Job 21:20; Isaiah 51:17; Jeremiah 25:13; Revelation 18:16]. In Psalm 75 it is described as 'full of foaming wine mixed with spices'. This is a reference to the spices which were added to increase its pungency. The NEB renders the phrase 'hot with spice'.)

In verses 9–10 Asaph makes a declaration that he will constantly proclaim the greatness of God, and work hard for social righteousness. These are two aspects of mission in our society that need to be kept together. Preaching is to play a prominent part in evangelism, but social action needs to be included also. We need both 'words' and 'works' in order to win the world!

## Questions

1. Why is it that the Lord seems to wait until the very last moment to step in and help?
2. Do we give equal time in our local churches to preaching the gospel and to doing good? In other words, do we place equal emphasis on 'words' and 'works'? Discuss whether our emphasis needs to change.
3. How much does it matter what others think of the church? (Look at Matthew 5:16 and John 3:34–35.)

# Psalm 76

## The Lord dazzles the enemy

**God is far superior to the rulers of the earth.**

Asaph obviously intends this song for use in public worship, since he addresses it to the 'director of music' (or 'choir director'). He directs this song to be accompanied by stringed instruments. Perhaps the tempo of the tune was better suited to stringed instruments, but we cannot say. However, from the words we can hazard a guess that the tune would be upbeat and joyful. This song is celebrating the splendour and majestic might of God: only celebratory music would be fitting!

The writer begins by talking about the international fame of the Lord. He is not only known in both Judah and Israel, his Name is held in the highest esteem (verse 1). Also, Asaph wants everybody to know that the Lord lives among his people. His 'tent' (verse 2) is to be found in Jerusalem. The writer refers to Jerusalem by using two alternative titles for the city. First, he calls it 'Salem', which is another spelling of the Hebrew word *shalom*. This word means 'wholeness, completeness or peace'. By inference he is saying that, where God dwells, there is peace and he resides with us!

The other word he uses is 'Zion'. This refers to the hilltop fortress that David captured, so making Jerusalem not only the city of peace but also the city of David. From David's descendants would come Jesus, the Prince of Peace.

Jerusalem is not just the place of peace because the Lord lives there; it is also his protected property. God defends his city against those who come to attack it with 'flashing arrows' (verse 3); literally 'thunderbolts of the bow'. He breaks all the weapons of war. His outshining radiance dazzles those who approach the city with mischief in mind. Here Asaph may be referring to an actual battle in 701 BC, when Sennacherib the

king of Assyria met defeat (verses 4–5; see also 2 Kings 18:13 –
19:37; Isaiah 36 – 37). The ground was literally covered with
corpses of the defeated Assyrian army. Writing about these
verses, Kidner (p. 274) says that the language may well refer to
this historic incident, 'as if to remind us that miracles are actual
and datable, not picturesque statements of general truths'.

The writer recognizes that Jerusalem was saved from the
ancient horse-drawn battle wagons by none other than the Lord
himself (verse 6). This was not the first time in their history that
God had stepped in to rescue his people from 'horse and
chariot' (see Exodus 14:1 – 15:21).

In the light of this divine splendour and power, it makes sense
to give reverence to the Lord alone. Not even the most powerful
enemy can stand against his righteous anger (verse 7). In the light
of his judgments, whole populations are stunned into silence
(verse 8). Asaph notes that the purpose of God's judgments is to
save those who have committed their cause to him. He seeks to
help those who cannot or will not help themselves.

Verse 10 is puzzling. How are we to understand this verse
which the Reformer Miles Coverdale renders, 'the fierceness of
man shall turn to thy praise'? It may be that it can only be
understood in the light of the cross. There, man's rage was pitted
against Christ. However, for those who come to understand
what happened on the cross, it speaks not only of man's rage but
of God's redemption. In the light of this 'saving grace', anger is
turned into praise (verse 10; see also Acts 2:23–28).

The writer ends the psalm by drawing an obvious conclusion
to all that has been said. If God is dazzling in his splendour and
incomparable in might, it is only common sense to fulfil the
promises we have made to him (verses 11–12).

## Questions

1. How far do our lives reflect the purity of God?
2. How can we show God's 'righteous anger' against abuses in
   society?
3. Why does the world prefer 'darkness' to light?

# Psalm 77

## When God seems to forget

**We need to look away from our circumstances and focus on God.**

The title directs attention to the 'director of music'. Asaph also requests that Juduthun, one of King David's chosen worship leaders (1 Chronicles 16:41; 25:1–3), should lead the congregation in singing this psalm.

The song writer finds himself in a desperate situation. We are not told exactly what caused this difficulty, but we do know that it could only be expressed in a desperate cry to God for help (verse 1). This problem was not only extremely trying for the writer because of its overwhelming nature, it was also severely taxing because it went on and on. Asaph prayed night and day, often praying with uplifted hands, a sign of utter dependency on God. Even this brought him no relief. He was sometimes unable to put his prayers into words, and could only utter a groan from deep inside himself. He was trying so hard to get through to God in prayer that on occasion he became dizzy and faint (verses 2–4).

The writer is willing to try anything to get his spirit to lift. He reflects back on happy times when he knew the Lord's favour. However, this process only leads him to ask why, if God could act on his behalf in former times, does he seem unwilling to do so now? Asaph wonders if God has suffered a bout of amnesia. Has the Almighty forgotten how to be loving, merciful and compassionate (verses 5–9; see also Psalm 13:1).

Like so many psalms when the writer is cast down, something seems to happen that changes his perspective on his circumstances. When we reach verse 10, Asaph's attitude suddenly changes. A number of commentators have noted that in verses 1–9 there is a preponderance of the personal pronoun

'I'. Depending upon which version you read, the first nine verses have up to twenty-two uses of the personal pronoun and God is only mentioned eleven times. This would seem to indicate that Asaph's vision was unbalanced. He was focusing too much on himself and not enough upon God.

In verses 10–20, again depending upon which version you are reading, there are only three personal references and in this section there are twenty-four mentions of God. The right spiritual balance seems to have been restored!

Now Asaph centres his thinking on a God who is able to perform miracles and work mighty deeds. God is a 'holy' God (verse 13). Here Asaph uses a formidable word, which conveys the aspect of God as one who 'lives in unapproachable light'. As Kidner puts it (p. 279), God is 'fearful as an enemy but glorious as a friend'. At the time of the exodus from Egypt, God 'redeemed' or 'purchased at great price' his covenant people. When they were being pursued by the Egyptian army, God made a path through the Red Sea. He even provided under-shepherds to help lead his people (verses 10–20).

In the light of this, Asaph's spiritual balance and confidence seem to have been restored. He had come out of the darkness of verses 1–9 into the light of verses 10–20. G. Campbell Morgan puts it well when he writes, 'The message of this psalm is that to brood upon sorrow is to be broken and disheartened, while to see God is to sing on the darkest day' (*Notes on the Psalms*, p. 64).

## Questions

1. How can we keep our gaze on God when times get tough? Make a list of suggestions.
2. How do we as local churches provide help for those who are dealing with doubt? How might we improve?
3. What does society think when it sees Christians able to rejoice even in times of trouble?

# Psalm 78

## When will you ever learn?

---

**God's people rebel, but he constantly calls them back to himself.**

---

This song is entitled a *maskil*, indicating that it is intended to educate the hearers. In verses 1–5 the writer encourages the listeners to pay attention to his words. He is going to talk to them using parables, i.e. any form of teaching that the hearer could 'see', with his mind's eye. So Asaph is asking his audience to picture in their minds what he is going to say.

He is going to pass on to them what has been passed down to him from father to son. Passing on to our children what we have learned about God is one of the Christian parents' chief duties. By doing this we serve a future generation, giving them an opportunity to know him for themselves. We also may help them not to make the same mistakes we have made (verses 6–8).

The word picture which Asaph gives us is not a pretty one. He begins with Ephraim (verse 9), the largest of the breakaway tribes who formed themselves into a separate nation following the death of King Solomon. The subsequent history of the Ephraimites made them a symbol of backsliding and apostasy (see Hosea 4 – 13). The cowardice described to us here was not that they ran away from the enemy but that they turned their backs on God. They literally forgot all that he had done for them! They put out of their minds that, by a series of miracles, he had led them out of Egypt and provided for them in the wilderness. This all seemed to count for nothing as far as they were concerned (verses 9–16).

After these evidences of God's love, provision and power, the people continued to rebel against him. They put God to the test, approaching him in a demanding and disrespectful way. They were treating him more like 'a heavenly slot machine' than a heavenly father. They were actively insinuating that God was a fraud (verses 17–20). Quite reasonably this made the Lord extremely angry. He had been the target of malicious character assassination. In response to this, God poured out judgment upon this rebellious people. At the bottom of this rebellion was the sin of unbelief, as is so often the case (verses 21–22).

## God, 'cut to the heart'!

The psalmist finds this obstinate defiance quite incredible in the light of God's generosity to this undeserving people. After all, he had provided rain, food in the shape of manna, and what we might describe as 'angel food cake' (verse 25). He had also arranged for thousands of quail literally to drop into the people's laps. They lacked nothing, but still they chose to rebel against the Lord. He in turn exacted a severe punishment upon them, taking the cream of their generation (verses 21–31; see also Numbers 11).

In spite of all that had happened, his people stubbornly refused to trust in God. As a result of this, many of them found that old age was a terrifying experience. If we leave God out of our lives, growing old is a lonely and terrifying prospect (verses 32–33).

With the shock of God's punishment came a return to him by his people. However, this repentance was often shallow and temporary. Despite their resolute determination to choose the wrong path and do the wrong things, God was more than patient with them. He recognized how prone to rebellion human beings are (verses 34–39; cf. 34–38 with Hosea 5:15 – 6:6, and verse 39 with Hosea 11:8 and 2 Corinthians 4:16).

The theme of defiance and rebellion is now explored again (verses 41ff.). In their rebellion during the desert wandering, the people had 'put God to the test' (verse 41; see also Exodus 17:7; Psalm 95:8f.). By doing this, they had 'vexed' the Lord. The Hebrew word translated 'vexed' could be rendered 'hurt' or 'provoked'. Their actions cut God to the heart! In the period of the exodus from Egypt, he had done everything to ensure their deliverance. The people, however, chose to forget all the Lord's past blessings (verses 42–51).

Asaph reflects back on how God had gently led his people

like a shepherd. Look at all the shepherding and caring words he uses to describe God's previous actions on behalf of his people (verses 52–55): he 'led', 'guided' and 'settled' them.

Even after all this care-giving exhibited by God, they still persisted in rebelling! They were disobedient (verse 56), disloyal (verse 57) and disgusting (verse 58). They turned from God to worship idols. These may well have been the fertility gods of Canaan. Part of worshipping these deities was to engage in sexual intercourse with the shrine priestesses. The people became like the so-called gods they worshipped: depraved and pathetic. No wonder God was so angry with them (verse 59). He had, after all, been betrayed in the way that a spouse is betrayed when his or her partner is unfaithful (see Hosea 1:2). Now we see words of rejection appearing in the text (verses 59–64): God was 'angry', he 'rejected' them, he 'abandoned' former holy places, he 'sent . . . into captivity' the symbol of his presence (i.e. the Ark of the Covenant), he 'gave his people over' to the sword (compare with Romans 1). He also withheld their joy (i.e. 'no wedding songs') and, finally, he deprived them of his word (i.e. no priests; see 1 Samuel 4:11–22).

In the middle of all this depressing defiance and turmoil, God moves into action. He has not given up on his people after all. Indeed, he comes to their rescue yet again. In David he even provided them with a skilful and honest leader. David gave up looking after sheep, and began looking after the flock of God instead (verses 65–72).

'Lest we forget . . . !'

## Questions

1. Can you give an example of a time in your life when you rebelled against God? Why did you do it, and what was the result? Are you rebelling now?
2. How do we know if God is angry with us? How might God show his anger with the church?
3. 'If we forget about God, it is not long before we begin to neglect his world.' What evidence can you see of the truth of this statement in our society?

# Psalm 79

## Knocked down but not knocked out!

---

**God's people may sometimes feel desperate,
but need not despair.**

---

The background to this psalm is probably the same as that of Psalm 74. In 587 BC, Nebuchadnezzar and his storm troopers attacked and took the city of Jerusalem. It was not only an invasion, it was also a desecration. They reduced the city to a pile of bricks. To add insult to injury, they also 'defiled' the temple (verse 1).

The writer describes in graphic detail the slaughter that took place. It brings to mind the heart-wrenching photographs of Cambodia's Killing Fields. In and around Jerusalem there were so many human carcasses that carrion birds fed on human flesh. Wild animals were disposing of the bodies that lay where they fell (verse 2). Blood had been spilled like water, and there were so many corpses that there were not even enough people left alive to bury the dead (verse 3). In the ancient Near East, to lie unburied was the final humiliation. It portrayed a person as one who had died unloved and of no account, 'as disposable as an animal' (Kidner, p. 286; see also Jeremiah 22:18–19). As if this were not enough, the enemies of Israel were taking this opportunity to pour more salt in the wound by way of ridiculing their predicament (verse 4).

The writer speaks for the devastated people when he asks, 'How long is this going to last?' Asaph senses that this tragedy has been brought about because the people have sinned against the Lord. The mention of God being 'angry' and 'jealous' here would seem to confirm this idea (verse 5).

In Asaph's mind, it would be more appropriate if the ballistic missiles of God's anger were targeted on his real enemies. It would be more equitable, as far as the writer is concerned, if those who were unbelievers and those who were responsible for this devastation were taken to task by God (verses 6–7).

It does not seem fair for this generation to suffer because of a previous generation's waywardness. What they need is mercy, not judgment. This mercy needs to arrive as quickly as possible for they are in desperate need (verse 8; cf. 'come quickly to meet us' with Luke 15:20).

In verses 9–10 Asaph prays, not for his people as such, but that the Lord's name would be held in high esteem. If the Lord were to step in and rescue them, then the enemies' taunts would be stopped and he would receive all the glory (verses 9–10). Following this plea for God's name to be honoured, the writer prays for his nation's prisoners-of-war to be reprieved. We know from Babylonian documents that Israeli prisoners-of-war were held in stinking dungeons, doomed to die. They were, quite literally, on 'death row'. Asaph asks God to use his strength and power to secure their release (verse 11; see also Proverbs 24:11f. and Luke 4:18–19).

The writer uses the number seven, the biblical number of 'perfection' or 'completeness', to describe what he believes would be the appropriate punishment for the Lord's army. He wants God to crush these people perfectly and completely (verse 12).

The psalm concludes with the picture of God's people praising him for his retribution on his enemies. This epic story will be told for generations to come. For although the people of God had been knocked down, they had not been knocked out (verse 13; see also 2 Corinthians 4:8–9).

Note: Although the psalmist prays in this psalm for God to take revenge on his enemies, this is not, I would suggest, an appropriate prayer for Christians. Read the following passages, and reflect upon how the Lord wants us to treat those who have hurt us: Matthew 5:7, 11–12; 6:12, 14–15; 18:21–35; 1 Peter 3:9, 16; 4:14.

## Questions

1. How do you respond when someone hurts you?
2. How could the local church help Christians who are

struggling to get over the hurt of broken relationships of various forms? Whose job is it: the minister's, the leadership team's, deacons', elders', yours?

3. The church often looks as if it has been 'knocked down', especially in today's secular, materialistic society, yet it is never 'knocked out'. Why is this so?

# Psalm 80

## Lord, smile on us again

_____

**A prayer that God will turn toward his people in grace and mercy.**

Asaph wanted this psalm to be sung to the tune 'Lilies of the Covenant'. This may have been a popular tune at the time which was to accompany songs that reflected upon God as the great 'promise-keeper'.

The background to this particular psalm could have been the division of the kingdom into North and South in 921 BC. Only Benjamin survived and stayed with Judah.

In this time of tension and uncertainty, Asaph composes a song that crystallizes the feelings of the nation. He appeals to God as the 'Shepherd of Israel'. In the past he has tenderly led and protected his people; now they need his help again. In the ancient Near East a king was sometimes referred to as 'the shepherd of his people'. For in the opening verse of this song, Asaph blends together both the caring and kingly qualities of God. He is the one enthroned in dazzling glory (see Exodus 25:18–22; Psalms 22:3; 99:1; Isaiah 6:1–6).

In his prayer, Asaph asks God to intervene in his people's predicament (verse 2). The writer asks God to 'restore' them (verse 3). The word 'restore' could be interpreted simply as a cry for help. It could also be seen as a request for God to 'turn to his people again', in the sense of 're-establishing' or 'deepening' a former relationship. The second way of understanding this phrase certainly fits with 'make your face to shine upon us' (verse 3). These words echo the Aaronic blessing which speaks of God's kindness and friendship shown toward his people (see Numbers 6:25). This phrase, in whatever way we take it, was important to Asaph because it occurs no less than three times in this short psalm (verses 3, 7, 19).

## Enough is enough, Lord!

Asaph now begins to construct an argument in which he hopes to persuade God to help his people (verses 4–6). He reminds the Lord that, when his people have prayed to him, all they have met with is his anger. How long would this situation continue? Reading between the lines, we perhaps can sense that the writer believed that his situation had continued for far too long already. He also describes the people as drinking 'tears by the bowlful'. This was not a healthy state of affairs. Lastly in this section, Asaph suggests to the Lord that the way he has been treating his people had led to them being considered a laughing-stock by the surrounding nations. You can also hear the psalmist hint to God that 'enough is enough, Lord; we need you on our side'.

In verse 7 we have the recurring prayer for restoration, only this time the word 'Almighty' is added to God's name as if for emphasis. Following this, the emphasis changes. God is now viewed not as a shepherd king but as a skilled gardener (verses 8–18). The people are now pictured not as 'sheep' but as 'a vine'. The Lord tended this young vine with ultimate care and skill (see Isaiah 5:1–2a). He prepared the ground for the vine to be planted. He provided all the shade and protection that it needed. The result of this careful attention was that the vine flourished and became fruitful. It spread as far as the Mediterranean Sea and the River Euphrates (verse 11). The problem was, however, that the vine produced bad fruit (see Isaiah 5:2b). This was the answer to Asaph's question in verse 12. The Lord had withdrawn his protection of his people because of their moral conduct and their unfaithfulness to him (see Isaiah 5:3–7). Without divine protection, the people were open to being picked off by any surrounding nation (verse 13).

In the light of this terrible state of affairs, Asaph asks God to 'return' to his people. He entreats the Lord to watch over this vine, which is as precious to him as a son to a father (verses 14–15; see also Exodus 4:22 and Hosea 11:1).

Changing the metaphor yet again, Asaph now reminds the Lord that Israel is his 'right hand' man (verse 17; see Exodus 4:22). The people have already experienced the anger of his rebuke. Now what they need is for his hand to be placed tenderly upon his servant people, and their loyalty will then be guaranteed (verses 16–18).

The psalm concludes with the refrain which we have noted has been gaining more emphasis as the song progresses. Now the prayer is offered not simply to God but to the 'Lord God Almighty' (verse 19).

## Questions

1. How does God 'restore' your life? In what ways do you need restoration?
2. In every generation God seems to 'restore' something that has been lost to the church. What has he restored to us in our generation? Are there other things we need him to restore to the church?
3. What restoring role can the church play in the world?

# Psalm 81

## Songs and sorrows

---

**A joyful song for a national festival. It also helps people to reflect seriously on their lives.**

---

The titles of the psalms often give us more information than we might expect. Take this song. Asaph entitles the tune 'according to the *gittith*' (see Psalms 8 and 84). The Hebrew  word *gittith* is the feminine form of the word 'Gath'. This is the name of a Philistine city, but it also means 'wine press'. The time of the grape harvest was a special time of celebration and festivity. It was also the time of year when the people of God celebrated the Feast of Tabernacles. This was the last of the three national festivals held in the seventh month of the Jewish calendar (see Leviticus 23 – 43):

▶ On the first day they celebrated the *Feast of Trumpets*

▶ On the tenth day they observed the *Day of Atonement*

▶ On the fifteenth day they celebrated the *Feast of Tabernacles* (or *Booths*).

At this last festival, the people remembered God's deliverance from Egypt. They made simple 'tabernacles' or 'booths' (shelters) and lived in them. This was to commemorate the wilderness period. A ram's horn was blown to commence the festival and to conclude it. It was a time of joy and celebration because of what God had done for them in the past. Then the 'book of the law' was read to them. So it was also an opportunity for serious reflection (see Nehemiah 8:1–18).

The psalm begins with a great shout of praise to God, such as might have greeted a king (1 Samuel 10:24) or celebrated a victory (Zephaniah 3:14). Then the command goes out to the temple orchestra or band to begin the music. The ensemble is told to start with the percussive instruments and then to bring in the stringed instruments (verses 1–2). The ram's horn (Hebrew *sopar*) was traditionally blown to commence this festival on the fifteenth day of the seventh month which coincided with the 'new moon' (verse 3; see Leviticus 23:23).

Worship does not depend on whether we feel like it or not. God *commands* his people to take part. In Hebrews 13 we are told to offer a sacrifice of praise (Hebrews 13:15). The word 'sacrifice' indicates that it will cost us something to worship. Worship, then, is a time when we give as well as get (verse 4)! Matthew Henry puts it nicely when he writes, 'No time is amiss for praising God . . . But some times are appointed, not for God to meet us (He is always ready) but for us to meet one another, that we may join together in praising God.'

Asaph recounts the story of God's miraculous rescue of his people from slavery in Egypt. He saved them from a foreign land and relieved them from the burden of trying to speak a foreign language. The slave master's tyrannical burden was lifted from their shoulders and they were released from having to carry heavy baskets of earth and rubble (verses 5–6).

This should remind us to record carefully what God does in answer to our prayers. When we are facing difficulties in the future, an accurate description of what God has done for us in the past is a real aid to faith!

In verse 7 Asaph speaks the words of God to his people. They were to be freed from slavery, but not from service. God releases people from sin, not to serve themselves, but to become servants of righteousness. He calls people out of slavery into a loving, and yet a disciplining relationship. The psalmist records that part of this discipline was the 'education by encounter' which they experienced at Sinai. There they met with the presence of a holy God and it was an awesome experience (see Exodus 19:16ff. and 20:18f.). At Meribah they discovered that God could withdraw his presence and leave them to fight their own battles (see Exodus 17:7; Numbers 20:13). Both these events were part of his loving yet firm discipline. In this regard the lessons for Christians are drawn out in Hebrews chapters 3 and 4.

In spite of all God's generosity to them, however, the people still stubbornly refused to listen to him (verse 11). In response to this wilful disobedience, we have the Lord's sad cry 'I gave them over . . . to follow their own devices' (verse 12). We could perhaps render the phrase, 'I had to send them off to stew in their own juices'. This is the sad and terrible truth: God will not force us to love and obey him. If we want to walk away in disobedience, he will allow us (see Romans 1:24, 26, 28).

## Questions

1. How do you ensure that you worship God whether you feel like it or not?
2. How do we as a local church demonstrate our dependence on God?
3. Why does God appear sometimes to let society 'go its own way'?

# Psalm 82

## The court is in session

**In the end, all justice comes from the Lord.**

The setting for this short psalm is the heavenly courtroom. God is presiding over a gathering of 'the "gods"'. Some commentators think that the picture here is of God, the great King, presiding over a gathering of unrighteous rulers or kings (see Isaiah 36:4). We know that in the ancient world rulers and kings were sometimes called 'gods'. However, perhaps a better way of viewing this might be to see God as the great Judge of a gathered company of judges, i.e. those who maintain the rule of law on God's behalf (verse 1; see Exodus 21:6; 22:8, 28).

These individuals (note the 'you' is plural) have been corrupting the law. The length of this tyranny, '*How long* will you defend the unjust . . .', should not be taken as God delaying in dealing with these wicked men. It speaks rather of his patience and desire to see everyone saved (see 2 Peter 3:9, 13, 15). These men have been upholding the rights of the criminals and giving them favourable judgments. At the same time, they have been ignoring those who really need the protection of the law, the weak and defenceless and oppressed (verses 2–4). The 'teacher' in Ecclesiastes sadly says that in a godless society we should expect nothing else (Ecclesiastes 5:8).

These unfortunate individuals' lives have been turned upside down by these crooked law-makers. They are wandering around in the moral darkness. For when the light of justice goes out in society, the darkness that follows is sure to be terrible (verse 5; see also Isaiah 59:9f.; Psalm 11:3; Hosea 4:6).

Asaph notes that these corrupt legislators will be brought under God's judgment. Even though they have been his so-called representatives, they will go the way of all flesh (verses 6–7). It may be that when the term 'gods' is used here, it refers to the 'principalities and powers' behind corrupt regimes as well as the human individuals who run them (see Ephesians 6:12; Isaiah 24:21; Daniel 10:13, 20f.; 12:1; Revelation 12:7).

The psalm concludes with a prayer for God to judge the earth (verse 8). If he is allowed to pass judgment, we can be confident that the right decision will be made. This prayer is echoed right at the end of the New Testament (Revelation 22:20).

## Questions

1. In what kind of circumstances do you find yourself praying 'How long, O Lord?'? Make a list and turn it into a prayer.
2. How well do we demonstrate God's patience with those who are yet to become Christians?
3. Should we pray that God will come in judgment, or should we pray that he will delay his coming for the sake of those yet lost? If you had the chance, what arguments would you use on either side?

# Psalm 83

## Blow them away, Lord!

---

**God will deal with those whose one aim is to destroy his people.**

---

This is the last of Asaph's eleven psalms. Asaph calls out to God to defend his people against a catalogue of their traditional enemies (verse 1). It could be that the background to this psalm is to be found in 2  Chronicles 20, when Israel was 'ringed by an unholy alliance dedicated to her destruction' (Kidner, p. 299). Or we can take it to refer to the continual attacks on the people of God throughout the ages. However we choose to interpret it, one thing is clear: the enemies of God's people are the enemies of God. Note verse 2 'your enemies' and 'your foes', and verse 3 'your people' and 'those you cherish'.

This confederacy is determined to achieve one thing alone – the complete destruction of Israel. To so blot her out that she does not even remain a distant memory (verse 4). It is an alliance made up of those who have traditionally hated Israel and all that she stands for. Various tribes and nations are mentioned, some of them relatives of Israel. Together they form almost a complete circle round Israel, cutting her off from human help. As if this was not enough, behind the scenes there was the great power of Assyria manipulating smaller kingdoms to carry out her plans. Eventually, all would be engulfed in her great empire (verses 5–8).

Asaph recalls past victories in order to stimulate his present prayers. He asks God to repeat what he had done to Israel's enemies in the days of the Judges (verses 9–11; see Judges 4:9 and 7:19ff.). In verse 12 the psalmist refers to the enemies calling the people of God 'the pasture-lands of God'. This speaks of God's ownership of his people. In the New Testament there is a similar stress on God's protective care of those who are his own. Look at these three examples of God's people being his possession:

▶ We are his *church* and hell cannot overcome us (Matthew 16:18)
▶ We are his *sheep* and he will protect us (John 10:27–29)
▶ We are his *temple* and he will indwell us (1 Corinthians 3:17).

Asaph now turns to the Lord and prays that God will deal with his enemies in a way that both demonstrates his great power and their great impotence. First, he encourages God to 'make them like tumble-weed' (verse 13). The word translated 'tumble-weed' comes from the Hebrew word meaning 'to roll'. It portrays a 'whirling motion'. Here the psalmist is saying to the Lord that he can scatter his enemies as easily as a whirlwind scatters weeds or chaff.

Secondly, Asaph turns to another metaphor and says that God can destroy his enemies as ruthlessly and as easily as a fire can destroy a forest (verse 14). Thirdly, he pictures a storm that would terrify the bravest man, and he asks that God might send such a storm to chase his enemies away (verse 15).

This all seems to be rather lacking in mercy. But is it? Although verses 13–18 appear to be a request for unrelieved judgment on the enemies of God and his people, there is a ray of hope for the would-be aggressors. Asaph appears to want these judgments to be enacted so that the enemies might be shamed into seeking God for themselves (verse 16).

## Questions

1. How often do you reflect upon God's past victories in your life in order to find encouragement? Why not start this helpful practice now?
2. How should the church act in the world in the light of the fact that we are God's possession?
3. What approach could we take which might 'shame' society into turning to God? Is this a legitimate option for Christians?

# Psalm 84

## Homesick for heaven*

**The psalmist longs to be in a place where he can really worship God.**

It seems likely that the person who wrote Psalms 42–43 also wrote this one. It talks of a spiritual homesickness, what the Welsh describe as *hiraeth*. This is like the English word 'homesick' but with 'a little bit extra of Celtic wistfulness and longing' (Cousins, see note 1 below, p. 6).

As the writer thought about the temple, he longs to be in that 'lovely . . . dwelling-place' (verse 1). The word used for 'lovely' here is one usually associated with love poetry. He is 'pining' (NEB) to be where he can experience at first hand the presence of 'the living God' (verse 2). He reflects upon the temple, but in his mind he thinks about the birds who fly around and live in the courtyards (verse 3). This is not as strange a thought as it might first appear. There are three possible reasons for his reference here to birds:

► The writer may have been reflecting on the gentle and generous hospitality of God. Just as these birds were welcome in the temple, so too were all those who seek his care and protection.

► The writer may well have been comparing the fragility of these birds with the great power of God as seen in these huge buildings erected for his glory.

► The writer may have been secretly envying these birds' privileged position. They had their homes near God's altar.

* The title for this particular psalm is one given to it by Peter Cousins in *Harvester Magazine* (August 1988), p. 6. I have included some of his insights in my exposition of the psalm.

In verse 4 the writer stops thinking about the birds that live in the temple and turns his mind to the people who work in the temple. For him the priests have an enviable position. He imagines how wonderful it would be actually to live in the temple. To be there every day, instead of just the two or three days when most pilgrims managed to get to Jerusalem.

Now the psalmist begins to reflect upon the joys of a pilgrimage to Jerusalem and the temple that is situated there (verse 5). The pilgrims find that they are refreshed and invigorated even in the most arid places (Baca, verse 6). Equally remarkable, instead of growing more weary as they journey, their strength seems to increase as their goal draws nearer and the sense of anticipation intensifies (verse 7; see also Isaiah 40:29–31).

The writer asks for God's attention and favour (verses 8–9). He simply wants to be in the place where time no longer matters and nowhere else holds any attraction for him (verse 10; see also Psalm 73:25 and Philippians 3:8). He sees God as his protector and provider (verse 11), and finally in verse 13 speaks of the blessings which surround all who personally put their trust in God.

Psalm 84 is not only in itself a beautiful poem; it also illustrates the place of the temple in the affections of God's people in the Old Testament. As John Stott notes, 'The Temple was for the Jew the most sacred spot on earth, for there in the Holy of Holies was the Shekinah glory, the visible manifestation of the presence of God' (Stott, p. 73). But how can we apply this psalm for ourselves? There are two lessons:

▶ For Christians, God's presence is not linked to a particular place. It is great to worship God together with other believers in 'a place of worship', but God can be just as real to a person who is absent because of sickness or old age. Our longing should be to meet with him, not simply want to be in a special place!

▶ In the final analysis, worship is longing to be 'with the Lord'. Peter Cousins puts this well when he writes:

59

Indeed Christians who read this psalm will naturally associate the 'dwelling places' of verse 1 with the 'many rooms' of John 14:1. Worship is the most natural of all activities for God's people and the longing to worship Him fully will not be satisfied on earth . . . As for the pilgrims on their way to Zion, many disciples today can witness to the fact that as they travel towards the heavenly Temple, they also find that difficult and hard experiences can be sources of refreshment and encouragement (Cousins, p. 7).

## Questions

1. How much time do you spend thinking about heaven? Do you think that heaven should be more of a reality to us than it is? What difference would it make?
2. In what senses may God be more present in a church than in a garden?
3. Is 'heaven' a useful concept in our proclamation to the world? Give reasons for your answer.

# Psalm 85

## Restore us, O Lord

**God's people need his renewed vitality.**

In the first three verses of this psalm, the singers are counting 'corporate blessings'. They are reflecting back over the past and recording all that God has done for his people. They tell us that the Lord has shown  them 'favour'. Kidner (p. 308) informs us that this word 'favour' is interesting: 'it speaks of deeming someone or something to be acceptable, often in a context of atonement' (see also Jeremiah 14:10, 12). The songsters also put together a list of very positive phrases to describe what God has done, including: '*restored* the fortunes', '*forgave* the iniquity', '*covered* all their sins', '*set aside* all your wrath' and '*turned from* your fierce anger'. These phrases work like a photo-fit picture. Together they show us that God has been treating his people with great care, mercy and grace. For this the choir and congregation are eternally grateful.

It seems, however, that these blessings were now becoming a faded memory. The people have moved away from God and his favour. They are again in need of restoration, and forgiveness (verse 4). They have allowed thoughts, attitudes and actions which cause God's displeasure to be once again a part of their way of life. They need to be revived. To be 'revived' is to receive the Lord's life, love and power by the Holy Spirit. It is to be invigorated and filled again with godly enthusiasm. The word 'enthusiasm' is derived from two Greek words that literally mean 'God in us'. To be revived, then, is to know again God's power in us and his pleasure for us. It is to know again the blessings of his salvation (verses 5–7; see Isaiah 57:15–16).

Now we move from a choral piece to solo voice (verses 8–9). The soloist describes how he is straining to hear all God has to say to his people. He notes that God promises 'peace'. The word 'peace' here means more than the 'absence of trouble'; it incorporates the thought of 'wholeness' and 'well being' into its meaning. This *shalom* of God is available to his people so long as they do not slip back again into foolish and wicked ways. From what the soloist goes on to say in verse 9, he is confident not only of God's power to forgive but also of his powerful presence. The glory of the Lord will not only be experienced in the temple but throughout the whole land!

In verses 10–13 we have the results of spiritual restoration and revival. The people of the land will treat each other in a right and faithful way. They will experience a bumper crop of blessings in their lives. Finally, the Lord is referred to as a king making his way throughout his domain. Wherever his presence goes, things that are wrong are put right, and things that have been bad are made good! (See also Isaiah 58:9–13.)

## Questions

1. What would 'revival' mean in your life? Can you face it?
2. What would 'revival' mean in your church? Is it ready for it?
3. What would a revived church mean to our world? How far can we ever expect to see *Christian* governments/states?

### In revival, God comes close

In verse 6 the psalmist writes, 'Will you not revive us again, that your people may rejoice in you?' A question we need to ask of ourselves and our churches is, 'Are we ready for what revival might mean?' It could make radical demands on us and our churches. Are we really prepared for that? Take a few moments now to reflect on the following statement about revival and ask yourself, 'Is this what I really want?' Dr James Packer writes, 'In revival, God comes close; the light of his holiness shines into the depths of memory and desire, highlighting the ugliness of one's own sins and making the burden of them intolerable. The conscience-cleansing blood of Christ becomes precious as never before, and the revival convert remains supremely sensitive to sin, both in himself and others' (J. I. Packer, *Christianity Today*, November 1988, p. 11).

# Psalm 86

## 'I need thee every hour'*

---

**In our loneliness, God can become a companion.**

 This psalm is the only contribution that David makes to Book 3 of the Psalter. The writer is very familiar with Scripture in general and the psalms in particular, for there are nearly forty quotations in this song that are taken from other psalms or from the first five books of the Old Testament.

As well as the liberal use of quotations, we also find that David uses three different names for God here:

▶ *Adonai* or 'Lord'. This is the name which dominates Psalm 86. It indicates 'absolute lordship', and by the use of it the singer shows his sense of submission and loyalty.

▶ *Yahweh*, the special word that is translated 'LORD', which comes four times. It reveals the singer's sense of God as helper.

▶ *Elohim*, the word for 'God', which occurs five times. This reveals the singer's awareness of the divine might.

David recognizes that ultimately God is in control of whatever happens in the psalmist's life. He confidently brings his sense of isolation and loneliness before the Lord. He is in need (verse 1). He can only ask that God treats him with tender mercy because he is feeling extremely vulnerable and fragile (verse 3). Finally in the opening four verses, the psalmist asks that God might 'lift up' his soul. It does not appear that he is

* Line taken from 'I need thee every hour', Annie S. Hawks' well-known hymn.

63

asking the Lord to take him out of his present circumstances, but to lift his spirit so that even in time of trouble he can know joy (verse 4).

The singer is relying on the God he believes will answer his prayer (verses 5–7). Notice that in verse 7 David speaks about 'the day of my trouble'. Even in the darkest possible moments of life, David rests in the fact that God hears and answers prayer.

In verse 8 the psalmist perhaps refers to the theoretical possibility of the existence of other 'gods'. Even if this were the case, they are nothing in comparison to the living Lord! However, it seems more likely that David is referring to 'angels'. Even the mighty angels are of little substance in comparison to the God who created them. Eventually, all the nations will finally recognize who God really is and come to worship him. Only he can perform the miracles of salvation (verses 9–10).

As David is taken up with the greatness, wisdom and authority of God, it seems appropriate for him to ask the Lord to give him some of his wisdom. He asks to be taught the path of real discipleship. He wants a heart which is totally given over to the service of God. For him, following God is not one among many options; it is the only option open to him. He is willing to devote everything he is to explore everything that God is (verses 11–13)!

David's troubles have not disappeared (verse 14), but he is confident of God's commitment to him whatever the circumstances (verse 15; see also Exodus 34:6b). He is to remain in his difficulty, but he asks God to share it with him (verse 16). Touchingly the psalm ends with the singer asking God for some small 'sign of your goodness' to doubly reassure him that the Lord of heaven will continue to be his friend on earth (verse 17).

## Questions

1. How do you show in your life that 'without God you can do nothing'? What does it mean?
2. If God ceased to exist, what would happen to your church?
3. What evidence is there that the church is anything more than a human organization?

### 'The heart' in the Bible

In verses 11–12 David speaks about 'heart conditions'. He asks God to give him 'an undivided heart' (verse 11), and in verse 12 he responds to God with 'all my heart'. Now biblically 'the heart' is more than a reference to 'the emotions'; it also refers to 'thought', 'feelings' and 'will', all brought to bear on some aspect of life. The Victorian preacher and writer C. H. Spurgeon describes a 'united heart' when he writes, 'God who created the bands of our nature can draw them together, tighten, strengthen, and fasten them, and so we shall be powerful for good, but not otherwise' (*Psalms*, vol. 2, p. 3). Spurgeon also says of the phrase 'I will praise you . . . with all my heart': 'Praise should never be rendered with less than all our heart, and soul and strength, or it will be both unreal and unacceptable' (p. 3).

Look up Romans 7:15–25 and James 1:6–8, and reflect upon what it means to have 'an undivided heart'.

# Psalm 87

## 'Glorious things of thee are spoken'*

**The time will come when even the enemies of God will be converted and drawn to his city Jerusalem.**

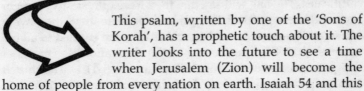

This psalm, written by one of the 'Sons of Korah', has a prophetic touch about it. The writer looks into the future to see a time when Jerusalem (Zion) will become the home of people from every nation on earth. Isaiah 54 and this

* This is the title of the famous hymn written by the ex-slave-trader, John Newton.

psalm lay behind Paul's words in Galatians 4:26 where he speaks of the heavenly Jerusalem.

The psalmist begins by describing the glories of the city. It has been established on the holy mountain (verse 1). The word 'holy' means 'special' or 'set apart from other things for a special purpose'. This mountain is holy because God chooses to dwell there. It is nothing in and of itself, but because he chose it, it is special and holy (see Deuteronomy 7:6–8).

When the psalmist speaks of the Lord loving 'the gates' of Jerusalem he probably has more than wood and metal in mind (verse 2). In the ancient world, the term 'the gates' often referred also to the people who congregated at the gates on all social occasions to hear the wise pronouncements of the elders of the city. The Lord loves the community who live in Jerusalem. For him it is more than a place; it is a people. This is also the case when we refer to 'the church' today. The 'church' is more than a building; it is the people who gather together in God's name. If Jerusalem is the place where God's presence can be experienced, then it is indeed glorious (verse 3).

Some commentators note that the phrase 'I will record' (verse 4) sounds 'official'. It may be the case that this was part of a formal proclamation on a state occasion. Whatever the setting, this is an incredible statement. For it lists not only Gentiles but also erstwhile enemies of the people of God as being accepted in Jerusalem as *bona fide* citizens! Egypt ('Rahab') is mentioned here, and Babylon. These were two of Israel's chief enemies. Nearer to home, Philistia is included. She was the enemy which Israel was never quite able to dislodge. Tyre is there to represent the affluent merchant-world, and Ethiopia ('Cush') represents the remoter regions of the earth. All these peoples were born outside the city, but they will be treated as if they were born inside Jerusalem!

People groups from all round the globe will have two birth certificates. The one will say that they were (physically) born in such-and-such-a-place. The other will state that they were (spiritually) born in Jerusalem and as such are entitled to all the benefits that this (heavenly) citizenship affords. This is a delightful picture of the church (Romans 9:4–5; 11:1). The church is now in possession of all the benefits of the 'new covenant' (Jeremiah 31:31–34). As Christians, then, we have two birth certificates: one states where we were born on earth, the other states that we have been born again to a new citizenship in heaven. This has all been recorded by God (verses 5–6; see also Acts 22:28; Philippians 3:20–21 and Revelation 21:24–27).

## Questions

1. How should being a 'citizen of heaven' affect the way we live?
2. How would you respond to the charge that our assurance that we are citizens of heaven is arrogant and unfounded?
3. Is it possible for Christians to be 'so heavenly minded that they are of no earthly use'? Where does the balance lie?

# Psalm 88

## The saddest song of all

**When we are totally engulfed by terrible circumstances, all we can do is to cry to God for help.**

Heman the Ezrahite (one of the tribes of Judah) was a founder of one of the temple choirs known as 'the Sons of Korah'. He was well known for his gift of wisdom (1 Kings 4:31). He was also famous because of his great singing voice (1 Chronicles 6:33) and his ability to play musical instruments (2 Chronicles 5:12–13). Perhaps Heman's great ability 'went to his head', and he became proud and arrogant. This inflated view of himself in turn led to his downfall, which is the background to this psalm. This is a nice theory but purely speculation!

We do not know exactly why this psalm was written, but someone has described it as sobbing with sadness from beginning to end. At first it does not look as if there are any signs of encouragement at all. However, the very fact that the song begins with the writer praying is a cause to give thanks. Perhaps he is in the depths of despair, but he is looking up to heaven for help (verses 1–2). There is little doubt that he feels that he is not long for this life. He believes that he is close to the grave, and the terrible thing is that there he will be forgotten by God (verses 3–5). The Hebrew phrase translated 'set apart' (verse 5) could also be rendered 'cut adrift'. This may be an allusion to the dissolution of all earthly ties in *sheol* (see Job 3:19).

Life for Heman is at a very low ebb indeed. He believes that he has incurred God's displeasure, and this sense of being out of fellowship with the Lord weighs heavily upon his soul. Not only does he feel that he has no friend in heaven, but he is grieving because he has no friends on earth. His companions have deserted him. Was it because of an illness that made his company distasteful? We do not know. But something about him led to feelings of disgust among his former friends (verses 6–8). Even here, though, he has not stopped petitioning God for his help. His hands have been continually 'spread out' in the typical posture of eastern prayer (verse 9).

For the writer relief must come for his condition before he dies. If he passes into the realm of the dead, his contact with God will also cease (verses 10–12). We must recognize here that the psalmist's view of the afterlife was limited. It was not until the New Testament era that these things came to full clarity.

In the last paragraph the writer continues his litany of woes. His prayers seem to go unanswered, he has been afflicted from youth, and his life is full of terrors. The psalm concludes with the melancholic phrase of a truly lonely person, 'the darkness is my closest friend' (verses 13–18).

## Questions

1. 'In times of trouble I turn to God.' Is this true for you? Can you give examples?
2. How does your church demonstrate to those who are going through periods of trouble that they are not going through it alone?

3. 'Honesty about how we really feel is a witness to the world.'
   Do you agree?

## Praying the Psalms

Heman may not have felt relieved by the time he had finished writing this psalm. Indeed, his circumstances seem to have changed little. He ends the song in 'darkness'. He may well have felt that his song was a waste of time. He would have been wrong to think that, for the words he penned here have been used by tortured and troubled Christians down the years. This psalm has given them words to express their grief to God.

This is an example of the Psalms not only being God's words to us but our words to God. We need to learn how to use the Psalms in prayer to help us express our deep feelings to the Lord. There is no need to 'hold back' when praying the Psalms in this way.

> The Psalms assume that when we talk to God punches do not have to be pulled nor words minced. Infinitives can be split and emotions expressed. There are hardly any feelings of pain, despair, vindictiveness, or let down that fail to be expressed somewhere among these 150 examples of things you can say to God (John Goldingay, *Praying the Psalms*, Grove Booklet, 1993, p. 12).

## Death in the Old Testament

In Psalm 88 we gain insight into the psalmist's view of death. He views death as (1) the opposite of life, (2) removal from the realm of living, and (3) the inevitable experience when life has been weakened by pain and weakness. The implication is that the experience of death puts human beings outside the realm of life where God acts in salvation and his goodness is known and proclaimed (verses 10–12).

This is consistent with passages elsewhere in the OT in which death is portrayed as loss of life. This is a mysterious and negative experience and yet a universal and all-encompassing one. The prospect of death is associated with feelings of terror, despair and hopelessness. There is no clear expression in the Old Testament of the New Testament idea that death is something to be desired as it brings release from this world and entry to something better (see 2 Corinthians 5:1–8; Philippians 1:21–23, although Job's words in Job 19:25–27 get close to it). Although the full Christian hope of eternal life is not developed in the Old Testament, however, there are indications that death is not viewed as the end. In fact, the Pyramids and other ancient monuments bear witness to the belief in some sort of after-life in most ancient cultures.

In contrast to the pessimism of the depressed author of Psalm 88, other psalms teach that death does not interrupt a believer's fellowship with God (see Psalms 16:10–11; 49:15; 73:23–26). This Old Testament hope, based on faith in God's ultimate sovereignty, means God is able to deliver from the threat of death (Job 5:20) and from associated feelings of despair (Isaiah 25:8; Hosea 13:14). Elsewhere in the Old Testament, the hope of resurrection is expressed even more clearly (e.g. Isaiah 26:19; Daniel 12:1–3).

## You, Lord, shall reign for ever

---

**God's rule is constant, even though his people are going through great difficulties.**

---

 Ethan is probably Jeduthun, who founded one of the three temple choirs (1 Chronicles 15:19; 2 Chronicles 5:12). He shared with Heman a reputation for great wisdom (see comments on previous psalm).

The background to this psalm is Nathan's prophecy to King David (see 2 Samuel 7:4–17; Psalm 2:7–9). The song begins with praise to God for his faithfulness and for the fact that he has established the Davidic dynasty for ever (verses 1–4). From the earth, the psalmist allows his mind to reflect upon how God is praised in the heavenlies. Even in comparison to the mighty angelic beings he is beyond compare (verses 4–8).

This God is majestic above the heavens and upon the earth. Only he can control and subdue the great power of the sea (verse 9). In the New Testament Jesus demonstrates his divinity by calming the waves. This dramatic action left his bewildered disciples asking, 'Who exactly are we dealing with here?' (see Mark 4:39). The sea is no match for this great God, neither are vast empires. The power of Egypt ('Rahab'; see Isaiah 51:9f.) is crushed like a delicate rose in a strong hand (verse 10). Kidner comments that this victory over Egypt is as central to the Old Testament as the cross is to the New (Kidner, p. 321).

God's creation demonstrates his majesty and strength. He is the one who made the great mountains of Tabor (1,900ft) and the snow-topped mount Hermon (9,000 ft). Even their great size is dwarfed in his presence (verses 11–13). God's rule is not only majestic, it is moral as well. The foundations of all he does are qualities like 'righteousness' and 'justice'. Those who learn to walk in his ways receive both his blessing and kingly protection (verses 14–18).

71

In verses 19–37 Ethan speaks of the covenant made with David. It was God who took the initiative in the selection of David to be king (verses 19–21). It was also God who promoted David to the high position he achieved (verses 22–27). In verses 28–37 the idea of a 'permanent appointment' comes to the fore. God would keep his side of the covenant even if some of David's descendants did not keep theirs. However, disobedience, even if it was found in a royal line, would not go unpunished. God's love is not sentimental. He will punish those he loves, both the high and the low.

The covenant cannot be broken. However, it looks as if it might be in verses 38–51. The king seems to have lost God's favour (verses 38–39). The royal crown is a symbol of consecration of both king and high priest (see Exodus 29:6). It has ended up 'defiled' and 'in the dust'. The city of Jerusalem is pictured as being captured and ransacked (verses 40–41; see also Lamentations 1:10–12; 2:8). The enemies of God's people seem to be in the ascendancy. A young king of David's line was taken into exile and the people were covered in shame (verses 42–45; see also 2 Kings 24:8).

The psalmist asks God how long will this state of affairs continue? If it does last for a long time, the fragility of human life and the threat of the grave will take their toll (verses 46–48). Ethan wants to know where God's former love and concern for his people have disappeared to (verse 49). He wants God to remember how badly he has been treated, and by implication he is asking God to act on his behalf (verses 50–51).

However, despite the darkness that appears towards the latter stages of this psalm, it does end on a note of praise. A doxology is followed by a double 'amen' or 'so be it' (see Psalms 41:13 and 2:19). As the third book of the Psalter closes, we are again reminded that God's people can praise him in the most difficult of circumstances.

## Questions

1. What keeps you stable in this unstable world? Make a list and be as realistic as you can.

2. How does your church exercise 'discipline' among its membership? Should it be stronger or more lenient in this regard?
3. Do you think the world really believes that God will punish the unbeliever? It not, why not?

### The purpose of God's punishment/tough love

Read Hebrews 12:1–13. Like any good father, God disciplines those whom he loves (Hebrews 12:6). In fact discipline is a sign that we are really children of God! We have seen in Psalm 89 that God was prepared to correct his people. This is one aspect of being a 'covenant people'. G. Campbell Morgan put it well when he stated that:

> To know the faithfulness of God is to know that when He afflicts there is meaning of mercy in it. When that is recognized, prayer for deliverance is proper, for it must inevitably be accompanied by a turning back to the Lord (*and turning away*) from those things which have been the reason (for) His punishments (*Notes on the Psalms*, p. 74).

# BOOK 4 (Psalms 90–106)

## Psalm 90

### Fragile people, eternal God

---

**God is solid and eternal; it is we who are transient.**

---

The fourth book of the Psalter begins with a prayer that may go right back to Moses. Although the psalms in this section are not specifically linked by name with the temple choirs (as were most of those in Books 2 and 3), most of them are intended for use in public worship. A general pattern appears to emerge:

- Psalms 1–41 (Book 1) tend to be personal.

- Psalms 42–89 (Books 2 and 3) tend to be national.

- Psalms 90–150 (Books 4 and 5) tend to be liturgical, i.e. concerned with the regular corporate praise of God.

- Psalms 90–106 (Book 4) tend to have God named predominantly as *Yahweh* (the LORD). Most of these psalms are anonymous, but Psalm 90 is attributed to Moses, Psalms 101 and 103 to David.

Now to Psalm 90. It could well be a prayer penned by Moses which has been preserved over the centuries and was an obvious choice to be included by the editors in the Psalter, (though this is not universally accepted). This psalm was the inspiration behind Isaac Watts' famous hymn, 'O God our help in ages past', one of the finest in the English language.

The song begins with a great statement about the security offered by God to his people and his awesome eternal nature (verses 1–2). God is addressed as both our sovereign and shelter. He is our 'dwelling-place'. This sense of security for believers compares with the 'cosmic homelessness' of those who have no faith (see Deuteronomy 33:27; John 14:1–4).

It is quite likely that the author was meditating on Genesis 1 – 3 when he wrote this psalm, for in verse 3 we have a definite allusion to Genesis 3:19. Here man is pictured as being 'from dust and going back to dust'. There is a story about a little girl who had heard a preacher say that we come from dust and go back to dust. One day she came running down the stairs saying to her Mum, 'Come quick and look! There is someone either coming or going right under my bed!' Dust speaks of the fragility of human life. It may well speak also of the futility of human life without God. One cynical writer states, 'Man is an empty bubble on the sea of nothingness.' Without Christ we humans are 'dust', nothing more!

The frailty of human life is then added to its brevity and compared to grass. It is annually renewed but always fading (verses 5–6; see also Psalm 37:2; Isaiah 40:6; 1 Peter 1:23–25 and Matthew 6:28–30). Man's life is microscopically short in contrast to the eternity of God. To God a whole millennium is equivalent to a day (see 2 Peter 3:8) or even to one of the watches in the night (verse 4).

In verses 7–11 the psalmist moves from God's awesome eternal nature to his awe-inspiring righteous anger. Our mortality is a consequence of sin (see Genesis 2:17; 3:19; Romans 5:12). Every sinful thought and action is laid open to the scrutiny of God whose searchlight penetrates the deepest darkness and the most hidden sins (verse 8). In this regard all the days of our lives pass away under God's anger, until we find faith in him (verse 9).

It has been said that there are only two certainties in this life: one is death and the other is taxes! We have to confess that death is indeed the 'ultimate statistic': one out of one people die. The writer recognizes this in verses 10–11. We may make it to seventy or eighty years of age, but we will eventually 'fly away' in death. The only way the prospect of death can be faced fearlessly is by having faith in the One who came to destroy the terrors of death (see Hebrews 2:14–15; 1 Corinthians 15:50–58).

## Three prayers

In the light of the brevity of human life, the writer offers us three prayers. The first encourages us not only to count our days, but also to consider the best way to use them (verse 12). These twenty-four-hour periods of time are limited in number, and we will want therefore to invest in them wisely. Only with God's help can this be achieved.

The second prayer is found in verses 13–14. The recurring phrase in times of trouble is 'How long, O LORD?' We do not know what the writer's problem was but it was severe enough for him to ask God for it to cease. The second part of this prayer is for God to 'satisfy' (the Hebrew could be rendered 'saturate') his people with his 'unfailing love' or 'covenant love'. If God answers this prayer, the result will be inner joy that will more than make up for the years of difficulty (verse 15).

The third prayer is to do with our life's work (verses 16–17). John Stott notes that, 'One of the tragedies of death is that it interrupts our labour and cuts short our achievement. This is true, however, only of human endeavour undertaken in human strength' (Stott, p. 78). When God is involved, any work has eternity invested in it (see Psalm 127:1).

Life is so short that without God it appears to have no real meaning. The atheist philosopher Jean Paul Sartre once wrote, 'Every existent being is born without reason, prolongs itself in weakness, and dies by chance.' However, with faith in God it can be a very different picture. Life, though brief, can be viewed as an opportunity to invest our time in things that will last into eternity.

## Questions

1. How often do you really think about how brief and how fragile life is? If you were to reflect upon this issue more often, how do you think it would change your lifestyle?
2. How well is your church preparing you for death?
3. How can we help the world to realize that there is more to existence than this life on earth?

# Psalm 91

## The song of security

**The believer can feel really safe.**

This song appears to be anonymous, but it might be a psalm of David.

It is a psalm that is especially relevant for all believers who find themselves surrounded by danger, whether from a human or a supernatural demonic source. The Jewish Prayer Book suggests that this psalm should be read before retiring to bed. We should not, however, treat this as an arbitrary guarantee that God will protect us in every circumstance of life. The devil certainly tried to tempt Jesus to claim the teaching of this psalm in a way that would have amounted to testing God (see Matthew 4:6; Luke 4:10–11).

Neither is the psalm to be claimed by a believer who deliberately steps out of God's will only to find himself in difficulties. John Stott puts it nicely when he writes, 'Only the children of God who are living in the will of God can expect the protection of God' (Stott, p. 80). Even then we are not guaranteed a life without pressure or pain, as we see in verse 15. What we can know ultimately, whatever our circumstances might be, is that we are secure in God's love. Psalm 91 is the Old Testament equivalent to Romans 8:31–39.

The psalm begins with the writer speaking to God (verses 1–2). He uses four words or phrases accompanied by four divine names.

▶ *'shelter'* . . . *'the Most High'* When we shelter in God we are literally 'above and beyond' those things or persons which may threaten us.

▶ *'shadow'* . . . *'the Almighty'* (Hebrew *El Shaddai*, see Exodus 6:3) The American writer Don Moen renders *El Shaddai*, 'Our fully dependable Provider'. When we 'rest' in the shadow of the Almighty we can be at peace. The Hebrew word translated 'rest' can also be rendered 'to spend the night', i.e. as in a hotel room (see John 14:2).

▶ *'refuge and fortress'* . . . *'the LORD'* (Hebrew *Yahweh*) We can trust in 'the LORD' to be our refuge and fortress because he is the living Lord, i.e. he is always present with us (see Exodus 3:14). He is also *Yahweh*, the covenant-keeping God.

▶ *'I trust'* . . . *'my God'* All that God is, is our personal assurance of security. His character backs up his promises.

In verses 3–13 the psalmist speaks to the reader. In a series of bold images he affirms the statement of faith he has made in verses 1–2. He lists a number of dangers that the reader might have to face: entrapment and deadly disease (verse 3); night terrors and piercing arrows (verse 5); pestilence or plague (verse 6); harm and disaster (verse 10); a crushing fall (verse 12); and finally attack by wild animals (verse 13).

Whether these dangers are real or symbolic, the Lord's protection is secure, just as a mother bird would protect her chicks (verse 4). God speaks of himself as a caring parent bird (see Exodus 19:4; 25:20; Deuteronomy 32:11–12). He is both tender and tough, able to protect his own as a shield protects a soldier. The Lord Jesus uses similar imagery about himself (see Matthew 23:27). In the end he was prepared to die in order to secure the lives of those he loves.

God's security also protects us from satanic attacks, and in verse 13 the lion and the snake are mentioned, perhaps as pictures of Satan (see 1 Peter 5:8; Revelation 12:9; 20:2). The New Testament has a lot to say about spiritual protection – both 'defence' and 'attack' (see 2 Corinthians 10:1–5; Ephesians 6:10–18; 1 Peter 5:6–9; 1 John 4:4; 5:4–5).

Finally, the Lord speaks for himself (verses 14–16). God will both rescue and protect the believer. 'Loves me' (verse 14) can mean 'hugs me'. The believer who finds himself in trouble is not guaranteed instant deliverance, but God's presence with him in the troubled times (see Isaiah 43:1–3). Those who trust in the Lord and acknowledge his name are guaranteed long life (verse 16). Their lives will span over into eternity.

## Questions

1. What does it mean in daily life to 'rest in the shadow of the Almighty'? How do you get there and stay there?
2. How do you respond to preaching that seems to imply that we are guaranteed safety, wealth and health as a right?
3. Where does the world look for its security?

# Psalm 92

## Praise: it's a sweet work*

---

**Praise is pleasant, not a chore.**

---

The previous psalm was about God's protection of his people; this one is about our response to his protective love. That response can only be one of praise! This is a song that was penned specifically for the praise of God on the Sabbath day, proof that in the Old Testament the Sabbath was a day not only for rest but rejoicing. It was intended to be a blessing, not a burden (see Leviticus 23:3; Mark 2:27).

The writer affirms the essential goodness of praising God (verse 1). It is both a delight to God and to us. To paraphrase what C. S. Lewis once wrote, worship is the very thing that God requires of us and at the same time does us good! Praise is also an all-day occupation. It should act as 'bookends' to our day. We begin and end the day in praise to God for his love and faithfulness – looking ahead into our day with praise for how God will take care of us, and looking back on our day with thanks for all God has done for us (verse 2).

As we have noted throughout the psalms, part of praising God is the use of music (verse 1). In verse 3 the writer specifies what kind of instruments may be used. The 'lyre' is translated from the Hebrew word meaning 'the ten'. So we have a ten-stringed instrument being used in worship. We also have a harp mentioned here. This is the instrument that David would have used to play to Saul when the king was in one of his foul moods (see 1 Samuel 16:14–23).

The psalmist now talks about the inner warmth of soul and the joy he experiences in his worship of God. God is great in

---

* This title is based on Isaac Watts' paraphrase of this psalm, '*Sweet is the work, my God, my King*'.

every way and deserves our praise (verses 4–5). At this point the psalm takes an abrupt change in direction. The writer is reflecting on the absurdity of observing all that God has done and then simply dismissing it. It is not that these people are not intelligent enough to grasp the facts of God's plans, power and purpose, but that they choose to not do so. It is not a matter of 'wit' but will.

This is still the case today. Some people, even after they have all the facts about Christ, still choose to reject his claims (see John 1:10–11; Romans 1:18–32). To be deliberately blind to God and his creation is to live at a subhuman level. The literal meaning of the word 'senseless' is 'brutish' or 'animal-like' (verse 6). The end of these people is not pleasant. They will be destroyed like useless 'weeds' thrown on the fire at the end of the working day (verse 7; 'weeds' is the way the GNB translates the word rendered 'grass' in the NIV).

In verses 10–11 the writer not only praises the Lord for all the natural strength he has provided for him, but he also prays for the continual renewal of spiritual strength. This may explain the use of the 'fine oils' mentioned here. Oil was in fact used as a symbol of the anointing of the Holy Spirit in the Old Testament (see Psalm 133:2). There may be an additional thought of preparing a 'living sacrifice' here, since the verb translated 'poured' is used elsewhere not for anointing but for 'moisturizing' the meal-offering with oil before presenting it at the altar (see Exodus 29:40; Romans 12:1).

The psalmist then uses two beautiful pictures of the lives of people who are 'right with God' (verses 12–14). First, he compares them to a 'palm tree'. This illustrates three very positive qualities of the Christian life: *uprightness* – the palm tree is tall and upright, i.e. it has dignity, and it speaks of a Christian's 'uprighteousness' and integrity; *usefulness* – the palm tree provides food as well as materials for making ropes, mats and roofing for homes and other buildings, i.e. it provides for others' needs; and *flexibility* – the palm tree is able to bend in the fiercest storm, i.e. it survives difficult times.

He also describes the believers as being like the 'cedar of Lebanon'. This tree grows strong and tall and lasts long. It can reach the height of 120 feet and have trunks of over forty feet in circumference. There are cedar trees in existence today that are estimated to be up to two thousand years old!

These 'tree-people' grow tall and survive because of where their roots are planted. For they go down deep into God (verse 13; see Psalm 1:3; Jeremiah 17:7–8; Isaiah 44:4). They will not only live long lives but fruitful lives (verse 14; see John 15:16). It should be our ambition as Christians to live for God over the longterm and to produce as much fruit for the kingdom as we can. We need to realize that we are left here on earth until we finish what God has for us to do (see Acts 13:36). If Ludwig van Beethoven could continue his composing until the end of his life, even though for the last fifteen years he was totally deaf, so can we continue to serve our Lord into old age!

After two beautiful descriptions of the believer the psalm ends with an inspiring metaphor for the Lord. He is described as the psalmist's 'Rock' (verse 15). This is a solid word, which speaks of God's dependable character and reliability.

## Questions

1. Do you really 'rest' on Sundays? How can you ensure that you do?
2. Does your church have a programme which will help you to 'keep on growing' spiritually even into old age? In what ways could such a programme be improved?
3. Where does the world look to find rest and relaxation? What can we learn from our answers?

# Psalm 93

## God reigns, OK?

**Because God is king, we can be secure.**

Psalm 93 begins a section in the Psalter which proclaims that God is king (Psalms 93–100, with the exception of Psalm 94).

There are two details to note before we get into the heart of this psalm. First, the Old Testament writers did not look back to an annual enthronement of God as did, for example, Babylonian religions. Secondly, it has been suggested that the kings in David's dynasty were re-enthroned each year. Apparently this was to remind them that only God was the true king. This is a nice concept, but it is not possible to say whether these annual re-enthronements ever took place.

The psalm begins by announcing that 'The LORD reigns'! Befittingly he is robed in kingly grace and power (verse 1). The Hebrew here has the ring of a royal proclamation like 'Long live the king!' A biblical parallel is found in 2 Kings 9:13, where the beginning of Jehu's reign is proclaimed by using the phrase 'Jehu is king'. Another parallel is found in Isaiah 52:7, which states 'Your God reigns!' The decisive tense of the Hebrew here points to the day when the king will come in power. This is a theme that is prominent in this section of the Psalms.

The concept of the coming kingship of God is picked up in the New Testament. In the 'disciples' prayer' found in the Sermon on the Mount (it should not be called the 'Lord's prayer', because the Lord could never have prayed a phrase like 'forgive us our debts [i.e. "sins"]'), Jesus teaches us to pray 'Your kingdom come' (Matthew 6:10). This speaks of both the desire for Christians to have God as the king of their lives, and for those who do not yet know his kingly reign in their hearts, to come to do so. This is so that his sovereign will might be done as perfectly on earth as it is in heaven (Matthew 6:10).

The psalmist sees the earth's stability as a natural result of God's established reign (verse 2). This is equally relevant for today's insecure world. Those who are not Christians are looking for what Alvin Toffler calls 'islands of stability'. These islands or oases of stability can only be found in God. In verse 3 the writer reflects on the forces which set themselves in opposition to the rule of God. Here 'the seas' are seen as symbolic of all that is hostile to God. However, it does not matter how powerful the seas are, God is sovereign over all and more powerful than anything else (verse 4). His Son, the Lord Jesus, demonstrates this same superiority over the troublesome stormy seas in Mark 4:35–41.

The last verse indicates that God is not only king and all powerful, but that he is also king and always perfect (verse 5). Kidner (p. 339) writes helpfully, 'Here is God's true glory, not of mere strength but of character.'

## Questions

1. What evidence is there that God is 'king' in your life? Is there enough to convict you of being a Christian before an unbiased court?
2. How are we as a local church proclaiming the 'kingdom of God'?
3. It seems today that the world *can* be moved by, for instance, nuclear warfare or global warming. How much trust can we put in a 'firmly established' world (verse 1)?

# Psalm 94

## O God, please show us your justice

---

**We need to see God's righteousness in action.**

---

Much of what the world knows about God is filtered through the lives of Christians. As J. B. Phillips writes, 'The laboratory-check for spiritual experience is life itself'. How are we living out the character of God in a watching world? Are we showing our audience just what he is like? Do we know what the Lord is really like and where he stands on issues of righteousness and integrity? We can discover a lot about the moral character of God in this psalm.

In verses 1–2 God is described as one who will not turn his back on wrongdoing wherever it is found. He will 'pay back' those who had the chance to do the right thing and chose to do the wrong thing. The psalmist asks him to turn his moral searchlight on those who prefer spiritual darkness.

In verse 2 we have the recurring theme of 'How long will this situation continue?' The psalmist wants wrongs to be righted because, while bad things go unchallenged, this gives the enemies of God and his people the chance to boast, oppress and murder (verses 4–6). It gives these people the false impression that not even God cares about what they are doing (verse 7). When we see arrogance, oppression and murder, as Christians we do not have the option to remain silent. Part of God's righteous judgment is achieved by his people speaking out against injustice. Dante wrote, 'The hottest places in hell are reserved for those who in a time of great moral crisis retain their neutrality.'

We are not simply to challenge issues, we are to challenge people as well. Those who the psalmist describes in verses 8–11 are adopting a bovine view of life. They are living in 'animal world' rather than a really human one. They are capable of better things, and the psalmist appeals to them to use their minds. Verse 11 is not intended as a slight on the human intellect. It is really a swipe at the precocious plans of unbelieving mankind. Their schemes will never stand the test of time (see Psalm 92:5; Isaiah 55:8ff.). Christians, then, should be at the forefront of encouraging people not only to use their minds but to use them with an openness to God and his Word.

In verses 12–15 the psalmist moves from the exterior world of his society to the interior world of his soul. He notes that he will be given 'relief from days of trouble' (verse 13). The Hebrew word translated 'relief' is an interesting one. It is often used of 'inward quietness' in the face of outward troubles (see Isaiah 7:4; 30:15). J. B. Phillips paraphrases it, 'His mind is at peace though times are bad.'

In verse 16 we have a call from the Lord for someone to stand his ground against the wicked (see also Isaiah 6:8). God expects us to 'put up' and not to 'shut up'. In an ironic way this is what the unbelieving world expects from us too. Albert Camus wrote:

> What the World expects of Christians is that they will raise their voices so loudly and clearly and so formulate their protest that even the simplest man can not have the slightest doubt about what they are saying. Further, the World expects of Christians that they will eschew all fuzzy abstractions and plant themselves squarely in front of the bloody face of history. We stand in need of folk who are determined to speak directly and unmistakably, and come what may, stand by what they have said (source unknown).

The writer knows that truly to stand up for the Lord is impossible without the Lord's help. This is true of us all (verses 17–19). The answer to the question of verse 20 is an emphatic 'No!' Only those who think like God can be on the side of God.

Even though there will be opposition to standing up and speaking up for the Lord, the psalmist has a quiet reassurance that he will stand and 'having done all, to stand' (verses 21–23; see Ephesians 6:13, RSV).

An elderly man with poor eyesight found it difficult to read the small print in the hymnbooks at church. One Sunday the congregation was singing the line, 'Judge not the Lord by feeble sense'. This man misread the word 'sense' and sang, 'Judge not the Lord by feeble *saints*'. In our witness to the world, we need to show in our lives the true character of God. We can only do this through the presence of his Son and in the power of his Spirit.

### Questions

1. In what ways do you 'risk' speaking out for Christ?
2. 'In a world with so many issues of abuse, the church cannot remain neutral.' Do you agree with this statement? Why? Why not?
3. Is it enough to make a Christian voice heard when people do not wish to listen? How far should we take action to *enforce* what we believe to be right? Give examples.

# Psalm 95

## Let's get ready to worship

**If we want to worship, we need to listen to God's word.**

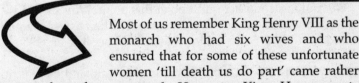

Most of us remember King Henry VIII as the monarch who had six wives and who ensured that for some of these unfortunate women 'till death us do part' came rather earlier than they expected. However, King Henry wrote theology as well! In his devotional primer, he calls this psalm 'a song stirring to the praise of God'. Psalm 95 is indeed a stirring song and it is intended to be so, for it is likely that it was used by a priest to call the pilgrim people coming to the temple to get ready to engage in the worship of God. It is sometimes referred to as the *Venite*, from the Latin word for 'O come'. In other words, 'Come let's get ready for worship'.

Modern scholars believe that this psalm was used at the Feast of Tabernacles. This was when the people of Israel remembered their time in the wilderness, when they were forced to live in temporary 'shelters' or 'tabernacles'.

Charles Spurgeon talks of this psalm in terms of 'church bells'. They are used to call people to worship the Lord on Sundays. This song begins with a 'call' or invitation to enter the Lord's presence with praise! Worship is best begun with praiseful songs, songs that express our love to him and our joy at being in his presence. It may be appropriate to 'shout aloud' to God as we remember his great reliability. Spurgeon uses a lovely phrase for this exuberant praise, he calls it 'holy enthusiasm'. God is the 'Rock' of our salvation. If we have placed our faith in God through Christ, our future is a rock-solid guarantee. Heaven, for Christians, is not to be hoped for but looked forward to! There are times to be reverentially silent in the presence of God (Psalm 46:10), but there are times when, if we do not express vibrant praise to the Lord, we feel as if we will 'burst' (verse 1).

Verse 2 encourages the worshippers to come into God's presence with thanksgiving. This should always be at the forefront of our worship, for we have so much to give thanks for. We are told here that we can give thanks and 'extol' (or 'lift up') God's name 'with music and song'. In this regard there is a place in our church music for both 'ancient and modern'. The real issue at hand is, who is the music really for?

We could ask another question at this point. Why should we involve ourselves in worship and praise? The answer is to be found in verses 3–5. We are to worship God because of:

▶ *Who he is*: He is Great! He is the great God and there is no other beside him. We need not take the reference in verse 3 to 'all gods' as being literal recognition of their existence. This is more a case of saying that, even if these deities existed, which they don't, the Lord would still be supreme.

▶ *What he has done*: He has made everything that we can see, feel and touch. He is the great creator (verses 4–5).

What is to be our response to these facts? In what Spurgeon calls the 'beating heart' of this psalm (verse 6), we are told how to respond. It begins with our *posture*. In the presence of such greatness, the psalmist believes that the only appropriate position is 'on our knees'.

We need to remember at this point that our bodies as well as our souls are involved in worship. Indeed, the 'body–soul' distinction, which has crept into Christianity, is more of a Greek (and unbiblical) idea than a Hebrew (and biblical) one. In Hebrew thought we are a unity. The things that affect me physically often affect me spiritually, and *vice versa*. The posture of our bodies can, then, indicate the attitudes of our hearts, truly humble before God (see Luke 5:8).

We should worship because this great God is 'our God' (verse 7). He is close to us in his goodness. John Stott writes, 'His majesty is tempered with mercy, and His glory with grace' (Stott, p. 84). We have here two sides of God's nature that need to be explored both personally (in our lives) and corporately (in our churches). For God is:

▶ *transcendent*, that is 'God far above us' in holiness and wisdom, *etc.*, and

▶ *immanent*, that is 'God right beside us', Immanuel, 'God with us' in Christ (see 2 Corinthians 5:19) and in the person of the Spirit (see John 14:17–21).

I believe that we need to have a balance between transcendence and immanence in our worship. This will keep us both scriptural and balanced. If we treat God in a too familiar a way, then our worship could be flippant or worse even irreverent! On the other hand, if we are always relating to God as a personality who is 'far away' (transcendent), then our worship may be in danger of being too 'other worldly' and thus irrelevant.

In verses 8–11 the mood of the psalm changes. From verses 1

to 7 we have had the praise of God at the forefront of our thinking. Now in verse 8 we are encouraged to think about God's judgments past and present. 'Massah' and 'Meribah' come in Exodus 17:1–7 and Numbers 20:2–13. They are landmarks, showing the beginning and the end of the unbelief that carried off the whole generation that came out of Egypt.

The centre of this unbelief was that they 'hardened their hearts' when God spoke to them. This is a very dangerous thing to do. The word 'today' tells us that it is still a dangerous occupation for present-day believers. Dr Howie Hendricks used to say that, 'It was far more dangerous to experience "hardening of the attitudes" than it was to experience hardening of the arteries.' The psalm that began in praise ends in pain. (See Hebrews 3:7 – 4:13 for a New Testament exposition of this psalm.)

There are always two things to remember when we come to worship. First, we should offer our words to God in praise but, secondly and vitally, we should also take time to listen carefully to what he has to say to us from his word in the context of worship. 'To listen' should lead on to obedience in the life of the child of God. To refuse to listen can only lead to disobedience and incurring God's displeasure. The sad consequence of this for the individual is to lack the peace of God.

## Questions

1. What helps you to enter into God's presence with praise?
2. Does your local church have a balanced worship where God is praised as being 'beyond us' (transcendent) as well as God 'with us' (immanent)? If not, how can this balanced approach to worship be put in place?
3. How can the church help the world to 'hear' what God is saying?

# Psalm 96

## Sing a new song!

**Coming to the Lord is exciting.**

After the encouragement of Psalm 95, worshippers are now ready for Psalm 96. They are to sing 'a new song' (verse 1, see also Revelation 5:9; 14:3; 21:1, 5). This is partly because of the 'hope for the future' that is expressed in this psalm (verse 13) and partly because, when God's people listen to his voice (Psalm 95:7–11), there are always fresh experiences of his grace. We are not intended to live on the experiences of our forefathers.

There is a place for 'traditions' in the church (see 1 Corinthians 11:23; 15:1), but there is simply no place at all for 'traditionalism'. In this regard Dr Jaraslav Pelikan once said, '"Traditions" are the living faith of those now dead, "traditionalism" is the dead faith of those now living.' Ours is to be a living faith because we serve a living God (see Matthew 22:32). God is the Great 'I am', not the great 'I was'. He is always contemporary and up to date.

### Revival and renewal

In every period of revival and renewal that the church has experienced, new songs are composed. Whenever God revives his people, they want to have fresh songs to describe their fresh experience of him. Also, 'new' songs say to the world and to believers that God is doing something here and now, not just hundreds of years ago. Every generation needs new songs to express its faith.

The term 'a new song' does not simply refer to newly composed songs, though it includes that, but it speaks of a response that will match the freshness of God's mercies, which

91

are new every morning (see Lamentations 3:23).

The second half of verse 1 urges the whole world to join in this glorious refrain. These new songs are not 'aimless ditties', they have a real focus (verse 2). They are filled with meaningful content, that is the praise of God and proclamation of his word to the world. Worship, then, has a vital role to play in the churches' evangelistic task. The late David Watson used to say that 'worshipping churches use evangelism to answer the questions raised by their praise' (see Acts 2:1–12). When we worship we celebrate all that God is and all that he has done. When we reflect on these marvellous deeds, there is no other option than to 'declare his glory' wherever we can gain a hearing (verse 3).

In verses 4–6 the psalmist reaffirms the solid reasons for worship. These are as follows:

▶ He is *worthy* (verse 4). In worship we give God his 'worth-ship'. The American writer Don Moen describes 'worship' as 'the atmosphere that welcomes God's presence and gives place to his mighty deeds'.

▶ He is *above all* (verse 5). God is 'real'; the other so-called 'gods' are nothing but fantasies. The word 'idols' is sometimes translated 'worthless' (see Job 13:5; Jeremiah 14:14). Our Lord is not 'worthless' but 'worthy', for he alone created all that there is. He brought into being both the earthly sanctuary and the heavenly (see Hebrews 8:5; John 1:14). Francis Schaeffer made the point that 'we become like the gods we worship'. If we are worshipping false gods, we will become like them . . . 'phoney' in our faith!

▶ He is a *splendid sovereign*, a *majestic master*, a *strong saviour* and a *glorious God* (verse 6). All these attributes build an impressive 'photofit' of a God who deserves our praise!

In verses 7–9 the psalmist uses the word 'ascribe' three times, just as the word 'sing' comes three times in verses 1–2. The word 'ascribe' could be rendered 'lift up'. The writer suggests that all the families on earth should lift up the name of the Lord, because of his incomparable glory and strength (verse 7).

The Lord's name is also higher than any other because of his 'shining character' or glory. In response to this we are not to be passive but proactive. We are to bring him an 'offering' or 'sacrifice of praise' (verse 8; see Hebrews 13:15). Lastly, in this section, the psalmist encourages his listeners to worship God because of his 'holiness' (verse 9). One way of thinking about 'holiness' is to realize that the Lord is 'totally different from any other person we know'. This should cause us to experience what we might call 'holy shivers' in his presence (verse 9).

God, the mighty King, is coming (verses 10–13). The nations need to know that the person who is really in charge of world events is none other than the Lord himself. What he establishes will remain (verse 10; see Psalm 93:1; Psalm 46:6). Now all of nature is instructed to join in this song of praise to the coming Lord (verses 11–12), for he will come and judge all the peoples of the earth and he will do this in a just and right manner. The standard by which this judgment will take place is the Lord's unchangeable truth, contained in his Word (verse 13).

## Questions

1. What are the values and dangers of tradition in worship?
2. How can your church encourage a new generation of songwriters?
3. How can we help the world to see that the Lord is not a God who 'was' but who 'is'?

# Psalm 97

## Friendship and fire

**For those who love the Lord, the 'day' will be one of friendship; for the godless, it will be a matter of 'fire'.**

This psalm is in contrast to the previous one. It begins with the recurring theme of God as king. Because of his righteous rule, the earth is made glad. Even the most remote corners of the world have cause for rejoicing (verse 1; see also Isaiah 24:15f.; 40:15; 42:4). However, just in case we are beginning to think of God in terms of a 'paternal pamperer', the psalmist reminds us that there is much more to God than just his fatherhood; there is also his fearsome nature (verses 2–5). The writer uses a number of picture words to try to illustrate this. God is so much bigger, more powerful and awesome than many of us realize. Words are used such as 'clouds' and 'thick darkness'. God is not captured by our limited intellect.

There are, then, elements to God's character that are simply too mind-stretching for us to handle! The psalmist's words are meant to inspire humble worship of an awesome God (see Exodus 19:16–18; Judges 5:5; Psalm 18:7f.; Isaiah 6:4; Ezekiel 1:4f.; Nahum 1:5; Habakkuk 3:3f.). When God allows us to see more of his character, it is a time to pause and tremble at the greatness of it all. The very foundation of God's rule is 'righteousness' and 'justice' (verse 2b). He always does what is fair, just and right. How many of our present-day administrations could even begin to make such a claim?

The writer then goes on to describe two destructive capabilities of God (verses 3–5).

▶ *Burning* (verse 3; see also Hebrews 12:29). Just as fire is able to gut a house, ravage a forest and scorch a prairie, so the fiery presence of God can consume his enemies. Like the devastation after a nuclear explosion, so are the enemies of the Lord when he has dealt with them in 'fiery judgment'. Even the apparently 'eternal' mountains melt like candles on a birthday cake in the presence of such ferocious heat.

▶ *Shocking* (verse 4). If you have ever been impressed by the 'pyrotechnics' of a summer thunderstorm, these are nothing in comparison to the 'high-voltage' power of the living God. In the light of this power, the people of the earth are reduced to shivering wrecks.

In verses 6–9 there is the same mixture of delight and dismay that we find in the New Testament predictions of Christ's coming, when 'all the nations of the earth will mourn' (see Matthew 24:30; Revelation 1:7). God's 'righteousness' and 'glory' are broadcast in the skies above (verse 6; see also Psalm 19:1ff.). This implies that no-one has the excuse of claiming that they are ignorant of God's character and conduct (see also Romans 1). All they have to do is simply look up and around; there is abundant evidence everywhere. People who choose to deny the existence of God and fabricate the existence of idols will become as worthless as their gods are useless (verse 7; see comment on Psalm 96:5).

In contrast, those who love God will rejoice because of the righteousness of the Lord's just regime. From Jerusalem ('Zion') and its surrounding villages of Judah to the whole earth, God's righteous reputation will be made known. There are no real rivals for God's absolute claim to rule. He is, after all, Lord of all (verses 8–9).

The psalm ends with a call for those who love God to allow their *beliefs* to be reflected in their *behaviour*. If we are really children of God, we should aspire to like what he likes and dislike what he dislikes. This will be the family trait for believers (Psalm 5:5), evil will be totally rejected, and goodness willingly received (verse 10). Christians don't have to hide in the dark (see John 1:5–7). They can walk in the light and experience, as a consequence, the real joy of peace in their hearts because they are at peace with heaven (verse 11). Those who are right with God can rejoice in God. The words of the Westminster Shorter

Catechism seem to sum up verse 12: 'Man's chief end is to glorify God and to enjoy him forever.'

## Questions

---

1. Has there ever been a time when you have been 'afraid' in the presence of God? Describe what happened and why.
2. Why does the world have difficulty in seeing God in his creation? Is there anything that the church can do to help here?
3. To what extent can people be frightened into the Kingdom of God? What effect do natural disasters have on people's belief in God?

## Burning and blessing, hurting and healing

---

In our comments on verse 5 we discussed the destructive capabilities of the fiery nature of God. This 'burning' aspect of his character is not purely destructive or negative. God sometimes allows his people to 'get burned' in order to bring about blessing. This is what the Bible refers to as a refining process. The analogy used is that of gold which has to be heated to incredible temperatures in order to burn off the impurities present in the metal. When the gold is heated sufficiently, all the impurities float to the surface and are skimmed off. On occasions God allows this refining process in his people's lives, both corporately and individually.

Whether the heat is turned up by persecution (sometimes referred to as 'the fires of persecution'), or personal difficulty such as financial reversal, illness or family troubles, the process is always painful. However, it has a positive goal in mind. The Lord wants you to become more like his Son Jesus. He loves his Son so much that he wants everybody else to be just like him (see Romans 8:29). So, in order to get rid of everything that prevents this in our lives, he has to place us in the 'smelter of life's difficulties' (see James 1:2–4).

When we emerge from this process, we are more like Jesus and more useful to God. It burns, it hurts, but the result will be blessing and healing! See Daniel 3:1–30 where 'burning' led to 'blessing', and Malachi 3:1–4 and 1 Peter 1:6–7 where refining fire (which hurts us at the deepest level) leads to receiving a faith that is purified and personality 'hurts' being healed. In these fiery moments of life, God has promised to be in 'the fire' with us. That is some real ground for encouragement (see Isaiah 43:2).

# Psalm 98

## It's a certainty!

**The Lord's final victory is so certain it is as if it has already happened.**

When Christians use the word 'hope', they do not mean by that some kind of sanctified, wishful thinking. When we 'hope in the Lord' we are so trusting in his character, reputation and reliability that if he says it will happen it is as good as done (see 1 Corinthians 13:13; Philippians 2:16; 1 Thessalonians 1:2; and especially Hebrews 11:1). 'Hope', then, is a very solid word that indicates that we fully expect the Lord to do what he promises he will do. We can stake our lives on it, and many Christians have done just that. We can also act now as if the promise is fulfilled, it is such a certainty.

As Psalm 98 opens, the writer praises God not only for things he has already done but also for those things that he will accomplish in the future. See Mary's approach to this in Luke 1:45 – 2:55. She accepted fully the words of Elizabeth when she said of her, 'Blessed is she who has *believed* that what the Lord has said to her will be accomplished.' Notice Mary's use of what we might call the 'past tense of faith'.

The Lord is seen by the writer as being both strong ('his right hand' speaks of his immense strength) and holy. God not only has the strength to do whatever he wants, but he will do it with pure motives. Lord Acton said, 'Power tends to corrupt and absolute power corrupts absolutely.' This statement does not apply to God. He is both powerful and pure at the same time.

Can governments around the world say that? Our politicians are often governed by the idea that the end justifies the means. In contrast to this approach, in the last century the 'Christian Socialists' stood up against what they considered 'parliamentary sleaze' (some things never change, do they!). They stated that 'if something is wrong morally it can never be right politically'. When it comes to the Lord, the psalmist is confident that his morality is never compromised by his programmes and procedures. He is powerful and pure. A wonderful combination to imitate!

This 'pure and powerful Lord' has *already* (again note the past tense although this is a future event!) *declared* his 'victory' (salvation) to the whole world (verse 2). This 'righteousness' is putting right what is wrong. Christians need to adopt this approach to society. Instead of complaining about all that is wrong in society, we need to aim proactively at putting these wrong things right. If we are known only for criticisms without constructive solutions, then the world will view the church as irrelevant.

It is out of a heart of love that God has acted to achieve our salvation (verse 3). D. L. Moody said that when he discovered that God loved sinners, his whole ministry changed. Bill Hybels of Willowcreek Church has much the same approach. He says that part of the reason for the success of his church (there are fifteen thousand in attendance at the weekend services!) is that the people who come discover that 'God loves them and so do we!' It was love that motivated God to bring us into the kingdom. It was his love in the first instance that set up the plan of salvation (Ephesians 1:3–10). It was the love of God that made the psalmist to see this salvation as already accomplished.

In light of this love and confidence that the believer can have, it is no wonder that he wants to burst into praise. Here the psalmist does just that. For all that God has done, for all God *will do* we want to praise him. This kind of praise cannot be done quietly. Notice the 'worship verbs' that the psalmist chooses.

▶ We will want to '*shout* for joy' (verse 4). On Easter Day in some churches the congregation is led in what has been described as a 'festal shout'. The minister declares 'The Lord is risen!', the congregation thunder back 'He is risen indeed! Alleluia!'

▶ We will want to '*burst* into jubilant song' with music, and use a variety of musical instruments to aid us in this process (verses 5–6). For some of our churches this will mean 'speeding up the tempo' of some of the songs we use.

This kind of celebration cannot be limited to us alone. All of nature must be invited to join in. The picture here is of the sea providing the 'thundering bass line', the rivers are providing the 'percussive element', and the mountains the 'harmony'. All this is because the people of God want to join with all of nature to praise a God who, when he makes a promise, it is as good as done (verses 7–9)!

## Questions

1. Can you give an example of a time when you were so sure that something was God's will that you began to praise him for it before it was fulfilled? Think of some more examples for today.
2. What evidence is there in the life of your church that God loves sinners and so do you?
3. Perhaps if Christians were more confident in what we believed, then the world would take more notice of us? Do you agree? Why?
4. If we tolerate those of intolerant religions, will they respect us? If not, does it matter?

# Psalm 99

## Perfect, simply perfect!

**God is not only powerful but perfect as well.**

The theme of this set of psalms (Psalms 93–100) is the kingship and righteous rule of God. However, the mood seems to ebb and flow. Sometimes these songs reflect God's people as 'lost in wonder, love and praise' and worshippers who exhibit unrestrained joy at being in the presence of God. In other psalms the mood changes to a sense of being overawed in the presence of a holy God.

Here, then, following the delirious delight of Psalm 98, we have a psalm that reverently reflects on how exalted and holy (perfect) God is. It encourages praise from another perspective. We need this kind of variety in our services.

In verses 1–5 we find that *holiness rules in heaven*. In response to this perfect reign the nations of the earth 'tremble'. God's throne is pictured here as alive and God is seated between the 'cherubim'. These are not the round-faced little children with wings that we see in some religious art. They are powerful supernatural beings, often associated with God's nobility, grandeur and holiness. This 'living throne is a flying chariot, fiery with judgment and salvation' (Kidner, p. 354; see Psalm 18:6–19; Isaiah 6:1–4; Ezekiel 1:4ff; 10:1ff.). Where God is present, the buildings shake as well as the people (see Isaiah 6:14; Acts 4:31).

The response to God's greatness is not only to 'tremble' (verse 1) but to speak ('Let them praise', verse 3). The Lord is not only exalted in the earthly city Jerusalem ('Zion'), he is to be praised by his awestruck people among the nations (verse 2). Why? Because he is perfect ('holy').

In verses 4–5 we again have this emphasis on the power and purity of God. He not only has more than sufficient *energy* to accomplish all that he wishes, he has the *integrity* to do it appropriately.

In verses 6–9 we discover that *holiness can be encountered here on earth*. In the past God has spoken to his people in a variety of ways. The common denominator is that he has always answered prayer (verses 6–7). Because the Lord could be trusted in the past he can be trusted in the present:

▶ In the *past* he heard and answered prayer; *today* he hears and answers prayer (see Hebrews 13:8).

▶ In the past he was 'a forgiving God' (i.e. continually bearing with the weakness of his people and forgiving them when they turned to him in repentance and faith); *today* he is a continually 'forgiving God' (see 1 John 1:7). But the psalmist reminds us that we should not misread this continuing forgiveness as a laxity about sin on God's part: he will punish those who obstinately disobey. However, his patience is an outworking of his mercy as he gives us time to come to our senses and return to him (see 2 Peter 3:9).

The psalm concludes with an exhortation to worship the Lord in his holy place, and because of his holy (perfect) personality. Three times the psalmist has reminded his readers that God is 'holy'. Repetition is one way of teaching truth. The truth here of the perfect personality of God is too important to forget.

## Questions

1. What difference should it make to our lives that we worship a 'holy God'?
2. How can the church reflect the holy character of God?
3. How can we begin to show unbelievers the meaning of holiness? What do they think it is?

# Psalm 100

## Reasons to be thankful

**Let us give thanks for who God is and what he has done.**

The Puritan Bible commentator Matthew Henry was well known for his praiseful disposition. He was always giving thanks in all circumstances (see 1 Thessalonians 5:16–17). An entry in his diary illustrates this:

> 'On the occasion of being beaten and robbed'. I am thankful to God that: 1. I have not been robbed before; 2. That I was robbed not killed; 3. That I was robbed not someone else.

No wonder people called him 'Thankful Henry!'

There is something of this spirit of thankfulness to be found in this short psalm. Psalm 100 both summarizes and concludes the section (known as 'homage psalms') that has gone before (Psalms 93–99). Its theme is the 'Praise of God as king'.

The psalm falls neatly into two parts. The first of these is a *Call to worship* (verses 1–3), perhaps sung outside the temple precincts by the temple choir. The second part is a *Call to thanksgiving* (verses 4–5), given by a choir inside the temple precincts. When the worshippers approached the gates, they were probably encouraged to continue their praise as they entered the courts of the temple. Imagine the drama and the spectacle of sight and sound as this took place. Israel's worship was visual as well as vocal – something that Protestant worship seems often to have forgotten!

Now let's move from the general to the particular. This psalm *starts with a shout* (verse 1). This prompts the question, How did some of our worship services get so quiet? As Vance Havner once commented, many of our church services 'begin at 11:00 o'clock sharp and end at 12:00 o'clock dull!'

Psalm 100 may start with a shout but it continues with a

*celebration of service*. In fact, the word translated here as 'serve' or 'worship' also denotes 'work'. In the Hebrew mind there is no difference. This attitude can make all the difference to that 'Monday morning feeling'. In fact, Mark Greene suggests that, if we understand our work as being worship, we will be able to say 'Thank God it's Monday!' (the title of his book, published by Scripture Union in 1997).

In verse 2 the psalm *continues with songs*. The psalmist encourages us to 'come before' God (i.e. into his presence) with 'joyful songs'. Little children naturally sing when they are happy. It does not matter whether you are a good singer or whether you 'could not carry a tune in a bucket', when you are in the presence of the Father you love, joy naturally spills over in the form of a song (see Ephesians 5:19). Charles Swindoll states that, 'The Spirit-filled saint is a song-filled saint' (*David: A Man of Passion and Destiny*, Word Publishing, 1997, p. 33).

In verse 3 the writer challenges us to remember three important things as we come to worship:

▶ *The Lord is our Creator*. In worship we remember his greatness in creating us and we tremble (see Psalm 2:11).

▶ *We are his people*. In worship we remember that we are his possession by 'creation' and 'recreation' in Christ (see 2 Corinthians 5:17). We also reflect on his provision for us and we marvel.

▶ *We are his pastoral responsibility*. In worship we reflect on his care for us and we are humbled.

In verse 4 the psalmist encourages us to come in to God's presence with the double graces of thanksgiving and praise. In verse 5 he tells us why we should worship in this way.

▶ God is good – everything about him inspires *gratitude* in the believer.

▶ He is unchangeable – everything about him inspires *trust* in the believer.

The psalm which began with a shout of joy ends with a

statement of security (verse 5). However, this security is only for those who have come to know the Lord as the Shepherd and their Saviour. Isaac Watts' hymn is a fitting way to conclude our reflections on Psalm 100.

> Let those refuse to sing
>     That never knew our God;
> But children of the heavenly King
>     *Must* speak their joys abroad (italics added.)

When you know God, it's hard to keep yourself from shouting about it!

## Questions

1. List the reasons you have for being grateful to God.
2. Why are some churches so afraid of 'worship getting out of hand'? Is there good reason for these fears, and how can they be dealt with in a balanced way?
3. What difference should the fact that 'we are his people' make to the way we live in the world?

# Psalm 101

## Deep down honesty

**David sets out for us what an ideal king should be like.**

Psalm 100 describes a perfect heavenly sovereign. Now David writes about a less-than-perfect earthly king. This does not mean, however, that high standards are to be abandoned. For in this psalm David sets out what he thinks an

ideal king should be like. He describes the model king in two areas of life: private and public.

## The king's private life (verses 1–4)

The ideal king has the Lord's qualities of 'love' and 'justice' on his mind all the time. Indeed, he finds himself singing about them (verse 1). He should want the qualities he sees in the character of God to become the qualities he finds in his own life. His love should be God's kind of love. It is love mixed with mercy. It is also love that can be relied upon. The word translated 'love' in verse 1 is the Hebrew word *hesed*, which speaks of 'Covenant-keeping' or 'promise-keeping' love. It is important that a king's word can be trusted. It is equally important for us believers today to be known for saying what we mean and for meaning what we say. Our word is to be our bond (see Matthew 5:37).

The other word that David uses in verse 1 to describe what God is like and what a king should be like is 'just'. The Hebrew word used here is *mishpat*, which describes 'a whole new way of looking at life' where justice and fairness are central.

The word that seems to summarize all this is 'integrity' (or 'blameless heart', verse 2). 'Integrity' is what you and I are like when nobody is looking! It is what Charles Swindoll calls 'deep boned honesty'. 'There is to be no gap between what I say and what I believe' (Billy Graham). In other words, for the Christian it should be a case of 'what you see is what you get'!

David recognizes that to live such a life will take:

▶ A careful and prayerful *evaluation* of what we do with our lives (verse 2).

▶ A careful and prayerful *avoidance* of anything that might compromise our lives and witness (verse 3). The ideal king would set before his eyes 'no vile thing'.

▶ This means that we should guard 'the eye-gate' to our lives. We cannot help but see some things that are not helpful. That is a fact of life. However, we can prevent unhelpful images entering our minds by carefully avoiding books, videos and films that present 'visual impurity'. We also need to guard 'the ear-gate' to our lives. What we listen to can seriously affect the way we think and the way we act.

▶ A careful and prayerful *estimation* of those people who have a real influence on our lives (verse 3). This does not mean that we are to avoid contact with non-believers. It does mean that we should scrutinize our closest friends' outlook on life to see if they are in line with what Christ would want.

The ideal king was not to be influenced by the ideas and agendas of those who do not love God, neither are we! It's a fact that we become like those we associate with and admire. Therefore we need to avoid 'deep and influential relationships' with those who insist on resisting the truth, i.e. those who are 'perverse' (verse 4).

## The king's public life (verses 5–8)

This same 'deep boned honesty' is to be conspicuously evident in the public as well as the private life of the ideal king (verses 5–8). Those the king chooses to have around him are to hold to the same ideals as he does. They are not to pass on doubtful information about others to a third party (slander). They are not to be so impressed with themselves that they look down on all other mere mortals (pride). The ideal monarch will recognize and reward those who are faithful and blameless by recruiting them into his service (verse 5).

David was expecting too much from a human king. The only person who could truly fulfil this 'perfect picture of kingship' was our Lord Jesus himself. However, God does expect us to live lives of integrity. This is not only choosing to do what is right, publicly and privately, it is also choosing to reject what is wrong in those two spheres as well.

## Questions

1. How important is it to be careful about what I hear and read? Why is this so? Can it work?
2. How can you ensure that your church has integrity as a core value? What does it mean?
3. Why is society in so much danger when its leaders have double standards?

## Influential relationships

At some time in the future I hope to do a series of sermons that deals with 'texts of the Bible that have been wrongly understood and wrongly applied'. 2 Corinthians 6:14 – 7:1 will be one of the first texts I shall deal with, for this section of Paul's second letter to the Corinthian believers has been greatly abused by some Christians. Indeed, if this text had a cold, a lot of sermons I have heard preached on it were in no danger of catching it.

It has wrongly been made to teach that Christians should separate from other Christians who differ on 'non-essentials of the faith' or who happen to belong to 'the wrong denomination'. It has been used to justify Christians separating from one another over such issues as style of music used, the number of communion cups employed, and the number of aisles in a church building. What Paul is saying here, however, is similar to what we have been learning about in Psalm 101. That is, as Christians we should not enter into deep and influential relationships with those who do not intimately share our own belief in God. Here are two examples:

1. If we recognize that *marriage* is the second deepest relationship we will ever know (after our relationship with God), it needs to be carefully thought through before we enter on it. If we are Christians, to marry someone who does not believe in God or know Jesus as their Saviour, is to set

ourselves up for a life of pain. We will constantly be pulling in a different direction and ultimately be arriving at a different destination.

God does not want to spoil our pleasure in life, neither does he want us to be lonely. He simply wants us to avoid the pain we will inevitably bring upon ourselves if we enter into a lifelong commitment with someone who does not share our faith. To be single and sometimes sad and lonely is better than to be married to the wrong person and to be thoroughly miserable. To be straightforward about all this, it is disobedience for a Christian to marry a non-Christian, and disobedience always leads to sadness and regrets!

2. Another application of 2 Corinthians 6:14 would be in the *business* world. What it is not saying is that Christians must always work for Christians. That is not practical, neither could we then fulfil Christ's command to be 'salt' and 'light' in a rotten and dark world (see Matthew 5:13–16). However, what Paul is teaching here is that, where we have a choice in the matter, as Christians we should not enter into a business relationship with someone who we know is going to require us to act in a non-ethical and non-Christian manner. This issue needs to be carefully thought through, and many congregations would appreciate teaching in this area.

# A withering touch, a wonderful result

**God uses our troubles to draw us closer to himself.**

We live in an age which is obsessed by health. 'Sickness' is the unmentionable word in most conversations, for it reminds us of both our own fragility and the brevity of life on earth. Today we believe that it is our right to be healthy and wealthy. Indeed, some Christians have taken this philosophy and 'baptized' it, proclaiming it to be a biblical theology! The Bible never promises us a trouble-free life here on earth. In some cases, for reasons beyond our understanding, God chooses not to heal, and some people we pray for do not recover.

What seems almost to be heresy to our contemporary society, and to some Christian groups, is that God can and does use illness in a positive way in the lives of Christians (see the book of Job; 2 Corinthians 12:1–10; Galatians 4:13). It is entirely possible to be right at the centre of God's will and still experience extreme difficulty (see Mark 6:45–52; notice that the disciples were being obedient to Jesus' command when they met the storm). Illness, then, or deep trouble may be part of God's will for us.

The title of this psalm tells us that what we have here is a 'prayer out of pain'. The writer was going through an excruciating experience. He is so wearied by his illness/troubles that he is at the point of unconsciousness. At this point he turns to the Lord. Pain can be used by the Lord to lead us to pray. This is not always the case, however. It has been said that, when difficulties hit our lives, we can become 'bitter' or 'better' – it all depends on the 'I' in the middle. Pain can result in us becoming spiritually gnarled, emotionally bitter; it can also result in a time of explosive spiritual growth. It all depends on how it is viewed and handled.

Pain is easy to speak about when we live 'pain free' lives. It is quite another thing to speak rationally about it when we are gripped by the merciless fingers of ongoing agony.

In verses 1–2 the writer pours out his heart in prayer to God. The temptation, when we are hurting, is either to 'turn in' on ourselves, becoming morbidly introspective, or to 'turn out' toward the world, looking for answers that don't include God. Both of these approaches ultimately lead to heartache and disillusionment. The best approach is not to turn 'inward' or 'outward' but to turn 'upward' in prayer.

In his prayer this sufferer tells God what he is experiencing. Again, it helps to unload the details of our situation on God in prayer. The psalmist's life seems to be speeding by as his days 'vanish like smoke' (verse 3). He has lost all heart ('blighted and withered like grass', verse 4). This could indicate that he has some kind of physical ailment or perhaps literally a cardiac problem, or it might mean that he has lost all his former enthusiasm and zest for life. He has lost his appetite, and either forgets to eat or has no desire for food (verse 4b). He has lost control, i.e. he can no longer quietly endure his pain ('loud groaning', verse 5a). He has lost weight because of not eating (verse 5b). He cannot sleep; he has given up trying to, and now at night he simply sits up like all the rest of the 'night owls', ready to join 'Insomniacs Anonymous' (verses 6–7).

In verse 9 he continues his litany of woes. He finds that he is crying all the time ('I . . . mingle my drink with tears'). But why all this illness, why all this upset? Verse 10 may give us a clue. It seems that the psalmist believes that in some way he has incurred the displeasure of the Lord. Because of this, his life is shrivelling up before his very eyes (verse 11).

Whether there was in fact some unresolved sin in his life we do not know. Sometimes God does use illnesses to grab our attention and to call us back to himself after a period of sinful estrangement. However, we should be extremely careful not to see all occurrences of illness and trouble as indicating that a person is experiencing God's disfavour.

It could be that God was using these circumstances to reduce the psalmist to the point where he recognized his utter dependency upon God. If illness could achieve this, then it was performing a positive task. For notice that in verse 12 the psalmist now has a new vision of the greatness of God. He has also come to appreciate the tender, caring love of God in this time of trouble. Interestingly the word translated 'compassion' has the sense of 'mother-love' (verse 13). So in this time of intense difficulty the writer has discovered that he can run to God as a compassionate mother as well as a tender father. He has also come to believe that part of God's plans are to renew, rebuild and restore (verses 13–16). In other words he has a new hope for the future.

Has something happened to this suffering saint? We are not told that his circumstances have changed. We are told, however, that he has a new view of things. He has confidence in both God's willingness and ability to answer prayer (verse 17). He believes that the Lord is a 'prayer hearing and a prayer answering God'. This important fact needs to be recorded for the encouragement of future generations (verses 18–22).

The psalm concludes with the writer speaking of his strength being broken. This may be one aspect of illness and trouble that God uses to benefit the believer. He allows difficulties to shrink our view of ourselves and enlarge our view of him (verses 23–28).

## Questions

1. 'Pain can draw us near to God or drive us away from him.' What is your personal experience of this?
2. Why is it that churches sometimes teach so little on how to handle suffering in a positive way?
3. Why is the world so scared of suffering?

# Psalm 103

## Restoring your spiritual passion

**Back to basics to renew our faith.**

This psalm has been among many Christians' favourites for many years. Its words inspired Henry F. Lyte to pen his famous paraphrase of this psalm, 'Praise, my soul, the King of heaven'.

It appears at first glance that David wrote this psalm because he felt on top of the world. After all, it begins in such an upbeat manner (verses 1ff.) However, David actually wrote this psalm because he felt that he was in the darkest valley. It was written by a man who was not striding along in the spiritual sunshine but groping about in spiritual fog. He could even be the anonymous 'afflicted man' of Psalm 102!

It appears that, prior to writing this psalm, David had lost his spiritual passion. His 'get up and go had got up and gone'. He had somehow lost his spiritual vigour. This is a more common problem than you might at first believe.

Gordon McDonald writes very honestly about this kind of experience in his book *Restoring Your Spiritual Passion* (Oliver Nelson, 1986, p. 11). He candidly states that there is no magical fix to this condition. He writes:

> Then slowly it dawned on me that I and scores of others were paying a terrible price for this search for some magical breakthrough. We were trying harder, working longer, breathing heavier, and getting wearier. And it was an unpleasant journey when it shouldn't have been. Other words that described such a trip are sour, stale, bored and numb. We would never admit it but we were tired of God, of faith and of people.

I believe that at the outset of this psalm David felt this way. He felt spiritually tired and jaded. McDonald describes this 'spiritual weariness' in this way:

> . . . it is not the honest tiredness of the body we all feel at the end of a good working day. Rather it is the weariness of a tired spirit, the state of passionlessness when serving the Lord had become a tasteless experience, where the power and delight of being a man or woman of God is missing (p. 33).

This was how David felt, but what did he do about it? First of all, he does something that might seem a bit strange. He talks to himself (verses 1–5).

In verses 1–2 he tells himself to praise God. He probably did not feel a bit like doing this but this is beside the point. There is no place for 'spiritual amnesia' in the Christian life. David begins deliberately to recall all that God has done for him – in the words of the old chorus: 'Count your blessings, name them one by one'. Here is where a journal or spiritual diary can be most helpful. If you record all that God does in your life on paper (or computer disk), you will be able to read about it in the future and it will inspire your faith.

David goes right back to the basics of his faith. He puts into practice the principle of 'remembering in the dark what he had learned in the light' – something which is always helpful. If we are spiritually weary, we don't need to go to a seminar or read the latest book, we need to go back to the basic facts about our relationship with God. This will stir our souls, as we consider all that God has done for us. Note the marvellous catalogue of spiritual blessings David records for us. God 'forgives us' (verse 3); 'heals' us and 'redeems' us (verse 4; i.e. 'bought us out of the slavemarket of sin'). He 'crowns' us, i.e. makes us as a 'child of the king', and has 'compassion' on us (verse 4). Finally he 'satisfies' us, and our 'youth is renewed like the eagle's' (verse 5). David is probably thinking here of the Lord's ability to enable those who follow him to remain constantly young at heart and, as Isaiah said later, to 'soar on wings like eagles' (see Isaiah 40:30f.).

Having reviewed in verses 1–5 what God has done in his life, he considers in verses 6–18 what God has done in the life of the nation. The Lord has always been willing to help those who could not help themselves (verse 6). He was not the God 'who had to be found'. He was the God 'who made himself known' to his ancient people (verse 7). Other world religions could be described as 'men looking for God'; Christianity is, on the other hand, 'God looking for man'.

Throughout the longterm relationship which the Lord has had with his people, he has shown himself ever-faithful, yet they have often shown themselves ever unfaithful. How has God responded to this wayward behaviour? With compassion, grace, love and a mighty 'long fuse' (verse 8; see Exodus 34:6). When the people sinned, God did not act as an overbearing parent, always accusing. Neither did he continue to keep the heat of his anger well stoked (verse 9). Indeed, God does not treat his wayward children in the way they deserve: they deserve death, he offers them life (verse 10; see Lamentations 3:22–23).

The psalmist is giving us a beautiful picture of God as the patient Father, the one who is constantly looking out to the horizon to see the return of the prodigal (Luke 15:11–32). His fatherly love is immeasurable (verse 11), his forgiveness indescribable (verse 12). He, like the father in Luke's story, literally reaches out and hugs his errant people. The Hebrew word translated 'compassion' in verse 13 could be rendered 'bends over low in order to hold to himself'. Like a good parent, he knows his children's weaknesses. He knows that we are temporary, fragile, easily destroyed, easily forgotten (verses 14–16). However, even if others might forget us, the Lord will not (see Isaiah 49:15–16). We might slip from other people's mind's but we will never be left outside of God's love (verses 17–18). We can depend on this because God is dependable (verse 19).

In this psalm David has told us why he has reasons to 'bless the Lord' (verses 1–5). He has also shown to those who listen why the people of God in general have reason to be thankful to the Lord (verses 6–18). Now, in the last of these 'three expanding concentric circles of praise, he encourages the whole of heaven to join in with this growing groundswell of praise (verses

19–22). The psalm that began with David's individual determination to praise God ends with all creation joining in exuberant praise!

Although David began this psalm having lost his spiritual passion, by the end of the song he seems to have regained some of his former enthusiasm. If we feel that we have gone stale spiritually, the way back to freshness is to begin again with what God has done for us, for others and for the world. Begin again with the wonderful basics of his love, patience and forgiveness. Before long, if we allow ourselves to meditate on these things, we may want to take up the words of the old hymn and make them our own:

> Praise, my soul, the King of heaven
>    To His feet thy tribute bring;
> Ransomed, healed, restored, forgiven,
>    Who like thee His praise should sing?
>       Praise Him! Praise Him!
>    Praise the everlasting King.

## Questions

1. What kind of experiences have caused you to lose your spiritual passion?
2. What role does 'teaching the basics' play in the life of your church?
3. What difference would it make to society to see a spiritually renewed passionate church?

# Psalm 104

## Nature: God's best advertisement!

**The great variety and vitality of all that God has made.**

'Many writers have been moved by the beauties and the wonders of nature.' We have already seen one example of this in Psalm 19. However, the stress in this psalm is not on nature itself, but on nature as an expression of the wisdom and power of God.

The psalm begins where the Bible begins, with its focus clearly upon God (verse 1; see Genesis 1:1). The writer immediately fixes our minds on the praises of God. He wants us to know that creation did not just happen. All that we see around us did not simply create itself. Behind creation is the wisdom of the great Creator God. The world and the universe is not the product of some impersonal force but the creation of a loving, caring Father.

The psalmist describes this wonderful designer. He is 'great', 'clothed with splendour and majesty' (verse 1; see Psalm 8:1). You almost get the feeling that the writer is struggling for words that are adequate to describe this creative genius. The Lord is then described as dazzlingly brilliant, the One who fills all of heaven and has nature under his own personal control (verses 2–4).

Next the psalmist catalogues all the marvellous things for which the Lord is responsible. It is he who is ultimately our provider, not nature. Note all the provisions that God makes for his world, his people and all his creation. In his wisdom, God has so designed things that everything is interconnected and depends on other things for survival. For example, the grass depends on the water to grow, the cattle depend on the grass for food (verses 5–14). The water also helps vines to grow, olives trees to flourish and wheat crops to develop. Why? In order that mankind might enjoy the blessings of wine, oil and bread (verse 15).

Water also allows trees to grow, which ultimately offer welcome shelter to the various species of birds. God has also provided the appropriate habitat in which the small mountain creatures can enjoy safety and shelter (verses 16–18). This again reinforces the thought that God is not only in control of his world but that he cares for the smallest detail of his creation.

There is a reassuring order about all that God has created. He has not left nature to be unpredictable. Night follows day and season follows season. Man can make settled plans only because of the way that God has made his world (verses 19–23).

All that God has made is a marvellous advertisement of his wisdom, creativity and generosity (verses 24–26). Everything created by God is totally dependent on him. Without him, nothing would exist; without his spirit, nothing would continue to survive (verses 27–30). This is a simple but profound point made by the ancient poet. He also reminds us that only God is everlasting. Nature will cease at his command (verses 31–32).

The psalmist ends on a note of praise tempered with a word of caution. Those who love God will enjoy a life filled with praise and joy; but those who choose to live without reference to the Lord face a less hopeful future (verses 33–35).

## Questions

1. Who do you really depend on to provide for your needs: your company, the state, your friends, your church or God?
2. How can we use the beauty of nature as a springboard to speak to the unchurched?
3. If God cares for even the smallest creature, how are we his people showing a similar care for his world?

# Psalm 105

## Faithful God

---

**Incidents that speak of God's faithfulness to his people.**

---

In the Christian church we have regular opportunities to reflect back on what the Lord has done for us. One of these is the Communion service or what someone has called 'the Lord's forget-me-not service' (see 1 Corinthians 11:23–26). In this service we particularly look back to the cross and what the Lord Jesus achieved for us there. This acts not only as a reminder of his love, but also as a refreshment of our love for him!

Psalm 105, a hymn of praise to God, serves a similar purpose to that of the Communion service in the New Testament. It is meant to remind the Lord's people of all that God has done, and to draw from their hearts a response of praise.

The psalmist begins on a high note of praise (verse 1). Notice how often giving thanks (or praise) is linked to proclamation. As we focus on what God has done for us, we find it impossible to remain silent: we have to tell others as well. Again, notice that singing has a high profile when it comes to the praise of God. Music and poetry are always closely linked in the worship of the God who loves colour, creativity and variety.

As praise should lead on to proclamation, so singing about God naturally leads on to speaking about God (verse 2). This is the natural approach to take: we talk to God about people before we talk to people about God. In verse 3 the psalmist encourages his hearers to 'glory' in the Lord's 'holy name'. We might render this by saying that he is encouraging us to abandon inhibition and to revel in all that God is and rejoice in all that he means to us.

The focus of the believer is always to be on the Lord (verse 4; see Psalm 27:4). It is from this constant gazing on him through prayer, worship and reading his word that we are able to appropriate his strength to be our own.

Now the psalmist challenges his hearers to remember all that God has done for them and their ancestors down the ages (verses 5–6). Look at the aspects of the Lord which the psalmist highlights here:

▶ *He is in total control*: he is the Lord (verse 7).

▶ *He is totally reliable*: he keeps his promises and covenants over the longterm (verses 8–11).

Next, from verse 12, the writer shows just how God kept his promise. In other words he uses history to illustrate his point. He shows how God took care of his vulnerable people, preventing them from being abused (verses 12–15); also, when famine threatened Israel, God 'arranged' for Joseph to rise from prison to palace (see Genesis 37 – 50), in order to provide for his people. All this is simply to show that his word can be trusted (verse 19).

As he leafs through the pages of Israel's history, the poet now comes to the saga of slavery in Egypt and the miraculous way in which God delivered his people (verses 23–38). The Lord even ensured that, although the people entered Egypt as paupers, they left it prosperous (verse 37).

In verses 39–45 the psalmist details what we might call Israel's 'post-Egyptian experience'. He shows how God continued to protect and guide his people (verse 39). He also provided food 'on the wing' and water in the most unlikely of places (verses 40–41). The Lord did all this because he remembered his promises to his people (verse 42).

Notice the way that 'joy' features here (verse 43). The Lord brought his people out of captivity into a place of celebration and rejoicing. This great deliverance on God's part was not quietly noted in some dusty history book, but rapturously acclaimed by the people of God. Here they celebrated release from captivity to Pharaoh and Egypt; now we celebrate freedom from sin and hell. Here, instead of 'silent worship', write 'shouts of praise'!

Not only did the Lord provide his people with the liberty they longed for, he also provided them with blessings for which they had not worked (verses 44–45). Has he not done the same things for us? All that we have in Christ, we have by grace (see Ephesians 2:8–10).

As the people are reminded of all that God has done for them, their natural response is to rejoice. At the Communion service, we are reminded of all that the Lord Jesus has done for us, surely our response cannot be different!

## Questions

1. Some people are more inclined to give 'shouts of joy' than others. How far is this a personality difference or a spiritual one?
2. Why is the Communion service so important in the life of the church?
3. What does secular society shout about? Should Christians share more of the world's legitimate pleasures or fewer? Why?

# Psalm 106

## How soon we forget!

**The history of Israel reminds us how we continually choose not to remember what the Lord has done.**

We have just left Psalm 105 on a note of praise and joy. This next psalm could not stand in more of a stark contrast. In the previous psalm remembering led to rejoicing, here forgetting leads to failure. Although much of the same ground is covered in these two psalms, the purpose is entirely different. The previous song was one of national celebrations; this is one of national lament.

The song begins with the character of the unchangeable God (verses 1–5). Although we can change in our affections like the wind, God does not. 'We change . . . he changes not' (see James 1:17). God always remains 'good' and loving; this never changes (verse 1). The Lord can always be relied upon to do what is right in a totally fair and unbiased way (verses 2–3). This is how we can approach God in prayer; we can be sure that if he has promised something, he will deliver (verses 4–5; see John 14:13).

This reliability and dependability of the Lord stand in stark contrast to the undependable character of his people! The psalmist notes how quickly they forgot what God did for them in releasing them from the captivity in Egypt (verses 6–12). The writer reflects with pathos, 'they did not remember your many kindnesses' (verse 7).

How quickly the people seemed to have fallen into what might be called a 'corporate amnesia' (verses 13–43). They not only forgot what God had done in the past, they also deliberately chose to ignore his advice for the future. When Moses was delayed on Mount Sinai, they quickly turned to other gods. It seems incredible, but it's true. Before we begin to 'tut' in judgment upon this wayward people, we should simply reflect how quickly we forget what God has done in the past and turn to the 'gods' of self-dependence and human wisdom.

The people not only forgot what the Lord had done and turned to other gods, they also grumbled against him. They were never satisfied! They were even willing to take on board the disgusting practice of human sacrifice. No wonder God was so displeased with them. Spiritually speaking, they 'wasted away' (verse 43).

Yet, in spite of all this rebellion and defiance on the part of his people, God still responded to them in mercy. He did not abandon them to their own devices, he listened to their desperate prayers for help. His great love even caused him to change his mind about how these people should be dealt with. The Lord also caused other nations to feel sorry for the plight of his people (verses 44–46). That's grace, that's mercy!

To conclude this sad psalm, the writer appropriately leads his hearers in a national prayer of repentance. In this prayer they ask that God intervene again to rescue his people, not simply for their sake, but that he might receive glory (verse 47).

This psalm that has reflected upon the dangers of forgetting God now finishes by reminding God's people to praise the One who never forgets. He is the same dependable character from generation to generation. In response to this, the people are urged to say a grand 'Amen', and the song ends with 'Praise the LORD' (verse 48).

## Questions

1. Why do we have such a tendency to forget God's blessings and to wander away from him?
2. How can the local church help prevent this 'corporate amnesia' and tendency to wander spiritually?
3. How can we help the world to see that God is looking for them (see Luke 15:1–31)?

# BOOK 5 (Psalms 107–150)

## Psalm 107

### Great love, wonderful deeds!

**The Lord deserves our thanks and praise. He had brought his people deliverance, healing, salvation, provision and blessing.**

Book 5 of the Psalms begins with the words which form the refrain of Psalm 136. In both psalms, the psalmist encourages thanksgiving by recalling specific examples of God's love in his people's experience. So worship and thanksgiving find their inspiration in the events of everyday life. This reminds us that God not only meets his people in the place set aside for worship, but also intervenes in real life experiences.

In verses 2 and 3 the psalmist reminds God's people that they are 'redeemed'. This term implies 'rescue' and 'salvation' – in this case from the hand of an enemy. This redemption has happened because a redeemer has intervened to turn his people's fortune right around (verses 33–38). The worshippers who are called to thanksgiving are those who live through the continuous experiences of God's works of salvation. It is firsthand experience of salvation which allows worship 'in spirit and in truth' (see Jesus' words which connect salvation and true worship in John 4).

## Four types of trouble

Verses 4–32 contain examples of various troubles which God's people have experienced. These may refer to four different groups of people or, more likely, four different forms of adversity which God's people have known:

▶ Hunger, thirst and homelessness (verses 4–9)

▶ Imprisonment and forced labour (verses 10–16)

▶ Life-threatening illness (verses 17–22)

▶ Danger at sea (verses 23–32).

All these troubles are life-threatening; together they portray human life at its most vulnerable. Some of these experiences have happened to individuals; others, such as slavery in Egypt, wanderings in the desert, and the degrading experience of the exile, have affected all the people together. There are some clues about the cause for such troubles: verses 11, 12 and 17 describe God's people as rebellious and sinful, and make it clear that God himself 'subjected' (verse 12) his people to the pain they endured. This is a clear reminder of the seriousness of sin in the eyes of the Lord. The good news is that this was not the end of the story.

## Four cries for help

Verses 6, 13, 19 and 28 are almost identical. The people knew they were in trouble, they knew whom to cry out to (the Lord who had dedicated himself to their preservation), and as a result they knew the delight of divine deliverance. This is important: when we are in trouble, too often we don't realize it. We go to everyone else but our Lord for help, and then wonder why we remain in our difficulties. God's people had to exercise their faith; their cries for help did this with simplicity and sincerity.

## Four responses of praise

Four further identical verses occur (verses 8, 15, 21 and 31). They call God's people to praise him for his love (*hesed*; see p.

126), which is the basis of his saving deeds. They encourage God's people to rejoice because of his kindness and his ability to do wonderful things. The love and power of God is seen in his acts of deliverance – which are a direct response to the expressed needs of his people. Therefore again the link is made between praise and worship and the experience of God meeting everyday physical as well as spiritual needs.

All this is re-emphasized in the final section of the psalm (verses 33–41), which summarizes the wonderful works of the Lord by listing ways in which God *reverses* the human condition to bring blessing. This will bring joy to the upright and will silence the wicked (verse 42). Verse 43 reiterates the sentiments of the psalm as a whole: consider God's great love. This is true wisdom.

### Questions

1. What aspects of your everyday experience are the basis for your worship today? Make sure you turn your answer into reality by actually worshipping God.
2. How would you describe the kind of worship that you usually take part in? Does it bring you nearer to everyday life or remove you from it? How?
3. How would you respond to someone who says, '"The wonderful works of God" are just another way of describing nature in its diversity'?

### The redeemed of the LORD

This phrase is used in verse 2 to emphasize that the Lord has acted to deliver or 'buy back' his people. The word was used of exchanges in the market-place and included the paying of a price. The term includes both being delivered 'from' and being delivered 'to', so there is a breaking with the past as well as a new beginning and freedom for the future. In the New

Testament, redemption means breaking with sin and beginning afresh with Christ. He is the redeemer, and his death is the price of redemption (see, e.g. Galatians 3:13–14; Ephesians 1:7; Hebrews 9:12; 1 Peter 1:18–19).

## Hesed

*Hesed* is the Hebrew word used for the Lord's love in this psalm. It means committed, loyal love, for it is expressed within a covenant relationship – an agreement formally made and guaranteed. It is not about feelings but about faithful mercy and favour. It is consistent, regardless of circumstances or merit, for it expresses deliberate and lasting commitment (see Deuteronomy 7:7–10).

# Psalm 108
## Great love, certain victory!

**God's love, faithfulness and glory are the basis of the victory God's people can know.**

This psalm is linked to the previous one through the theme of God's love (verse 4) but its content is borrowed from two other psalms. Verses 1–5 come directly from Psalm 57:7–11, and verses 6–13 repeat Psalm 60:5–12 (although in the original language, there are a few minor differences between this psalm and its two sources).

Verses 1–5 show us that David is able to remain steady in the middle of awful circumstances because of one fact. He is certain that God loves him. Knowing this means that nothing can happen to him which is outside God's agenda for his life. This assurance is not something to keep quiet about. Indeed, it is the kind of thing that praise songs are made of. The music which comes from a grateful heart is the sort the whole world wants to hear. It can even reach heaven itself.

In verse 6 David appeals to God to demonstrate his strength on his people's behalf. The use of the phrase 'with your right hand' indicates the power of God (verse 5). He believes that his request will be answered because the Lord's motivation to help is his love.

In verses 7–13 we find David's prayer on behalf of himself and his nation answered. The Lord speaks in a clear and direct way, and his proclamation brings words of great comfort. The very fact that he is willing to speak to his people is a sure sign that any fracture in his relationship with them has been healed.

The Lord says that it is he who is in control of the nations. To him they are little more than accessories. The implication here is that, if the people of God trusted him more, they would not depend on their own strength to deal with these international situations. The Lord has already shown them what happens when they are left to their own devices . . . If he does not help them, they are hopeless (verse 12).

The important question here is, Why are these two sections from Psalms 57 and 60 linked together in this psalm? First, there is a theological reason: as we reflect on the character of God described and praised in verses 1–5, we gain fresh confidence about the certainty of God's victory, and then we can express the faith found in verses 6–13.

Secondly, there is a practical reason: the Psalms were the worship book of God's people, reflecting their developing awareness of God. God's people often re-used well-known words from existing psalms and applied them to new situations. In this case, the result is that two separate passages are joined together. Sometimes people are put off by such repetition in the text, and wonder how it fits into the scheme of the reliability of God's word. But this is to miss the point. The lesson from this psalm is that God's word can speak to us in fresh ways, over and over again.

## Questions

---

1. What particular challenge do you face today? What aspect of God's character gives you confidence to face that challenge?
2. Have you recently experienced God's word speaking directly into your life in a new way? Share your experiences in your group.
3. In the light of verse 3, how would you justify to a Muslim or Hindu the Christian's duty to witness to God as we know him? Do they have a similar duty? How can these duties be reconciled?

# Psalm 109

## Help, Lord, everyone's against me!

---

**When other people turn against us and show us hatred and rejection, the Lord can be trusted to stand beside us.**

---

What upsets you most in life? When have you felt most hurt or alone? In my experience it has been when it seems that everyone is against me. Sometimes our feelings are over-  exaggerated, at other times we are totally justified in our hurt. It is particularly upsetting when we feel that we are being unjustly accused of something, when we are being excluded by false accusations. In these circumstances, whether in the school playground, the work place, the family circle or even in the church, we feel the pain of rejection, isolation, injustice and even hatred, rather than the acceptance, companionship, fairness and love which we all crave. This is how the psalmist felt when he wrote this psalm. By ill-conceived attitudes (verse 5), words (verse 2) and deeds (verse 25), other people had worn him down until he was ill and could say 'my heart is wounded within me' (verse 22).

This psalm reminds us of the dire consequence of false accusations and hatred. We should remember this when we are tempted to 'run down' other people. But there is another lesson here. The psalmist is aware that the Lord loves to bless even those who are deeply wounded by others.

### Lord, do something – I need you to!

The psalmist asks God to help him and explains the reason (verses 1–5). In his misery he feels that God has been inactive ('silent', verse 1). (Note, however, that silence can describe God's *apparent* lack of intervention, which often precedes his timely intervention, e.g. see Isaiah 42:14.) Those who oppose the writer are referred to as 'wicked and deceitful' accusers, who have used slanderous words to intimidate him. This is the exact opposite of what the psalmist deserved (verses 4–5). He has offered prayer for them, and has been good to them by offering friendship, but they have responded with evil and hatred. What more could the psalmist do? He has come to the end of his human resources. 'Now God,' he is saying 'it's up to you.'

### Lord, show your justice – they deserve it!

The next section (verses 6–15) is surprisingly bold, and to some people it contains an unacceptable level of vindictiveness. It presents a series of curses which the psalmist wishes will come upon his opponents. He is in no doubt that he wishes his enemies to suffer as he has suffered, not least in the sense of knowing the trauma of accusation (verse 6). Curses are sayings which express the desire that others will suffer, and the psalmist clearly wishes that this will be the lot of his enemies (from whom he appears to single out just one). He desires that they will know short lives, trouble and insecurity in their families, financial ruin, and punishment from God because of their sins. This last sentiment, repeated in verses 14 and 15, is perhaps the clue to the way in which these curses can most helpfully be interpreted. Rather than represent the psalmist's vindictive nature, they express faith and hope in the outworking of *justice*.

God's justice includes the idea of wrongs being put right. It means that the punishment will fit the crime, for God will not and cannot overlook sin. This is why the psalmist can curse his enemies. His enemies deny justice, goodness and love, and therefore the psalmist is confident that God will not commit himself to their preservation. This is repeated in verses 16–20. The psalmist requests that God will repay his accusers (verse 20); this is God's responsibility, and part of his commitment to his own people (e.g. Psalm 135:14 'the LORD will vindicate his people'). It is the understanding of the requirements of God's justice that makes sense of the ministry of Jesus and motivates Christian lifestyle. In realizing that we can never meet God's standard, we become dependent on forgiveness in Christ.

### Lord, help me – I'm finished!

Verse 21 (and then verse 26) returns to the theme of God's love which has featured in the previous two psalms. Knowing God's love enables the psalmist to spell out his needs before the Lord. In the certainty of such love, he is at liberty to explain exactly how he feels – poor, needy, wounded, weak and worthless. This is a cry from the heart that doesn't hold back. It is the sort of openness you might only be able to share with a partner or very close friend when you are confident of their love for you and know they will try to help you. Once more, God's love and deliverance are connected. God's love is love that acts for the good – just what the doctor ordered for the psalmist's frail condition!

### Lord, do something – save and bless me!

Verses 26–31 are the climax to the psalm. The Lord is highlighted: his nature is to save and bless. He stands at the psalmist's 'right hand' in order to save (verse 31), in contrast to the accuser who stands at the 'right hand' in order to condemn (verse 6). But here is another emphasis too: Help *me*! The psalmist is declaring his faith in his special position before God:

he is the Lord's servant (verse 28), and therefore the object of his love (verse 26).

There are no 'Why me?' sentiments here, just a realization that being God's servant does not exclude us from the painful experiences of life. Instead, within them we can find our faith deepened and refreshed through new experiences of God's love and blessing. The result is that the honour of God's name might be extended ('Let them know . . . that you, O LORD, have done it', verse 27), and that we might actually experience joy again (verse 28).

## Questions

1. What pain have you experienced? How has it affected your relationship with other people and with God? Are you able to talk about your painful experiences with God or with others?
2. How do you feel about those who cause you trouble or have wounded you? How do you respond to them? How do you pray for them?
3. What does this psalm imply about the sort of person who is always accusing and running down other people? (Proverbs 10:11–21 has some further ideas.)

# Psalm 110

## The Lord God is Lord of all

**The purposes of God are established. He appoints a man to be king and priest over his kingdom for ever.**

This psalm is used frequently and in different ways in the New Testament (see Matthew 24:22; 26:64; Mark 12:36; 14:62; 16:19; Luke 20:42f.; 22:66; Acts 2:24f.; 1 Corinthians 15:25; Hebrews 1:14; 5:6; 7:17, 21; 10:13).

In its Old Testament context, it is best understood as a 'royal' psalm – a poem or song associated with an event in the life of a king of Judah. As verse 1 calls the king to take up his place of honour, it makes sense to link this psalm with a coronation ceremony. Anticipation then grew for a perfect king, who would satisfy the highest expectations and not bring disappointment. This anticipation led to the messianic interpretation of this psalm, which the New Testament writers endorse.

### Rule with me (verses 1–3)

The prophets often use the words 'the LORD says', so this whole psalm may well have been a prophecy. God instructs the king to sit at his 'right hand'. This suggests that the Lord respects the king's status, but also that the king is the Lord's helper (cf. verse 5, where the Lord is the king's helper). The Lord is establishing a unique relationship between himself and the king. God and king are fellow workers, though what is achieved is the Lord's doing.

The consequences of this are far-reaching (verses 2–3):

▶ The king's power will be recognized (the 'sceptre' is a symbol of power and authority)

▶ The king will overcome his enemies

▶ The king's own people will count it an honour to be in his army

▶ The king will be renewed in splendour, and will be refreshed (refreshment is frequently the meaning of imagery about 'the dew').

What a reminder, and what a promise to the king at the start of his reign! The Lord is saying: 'All you are and all you will do is my doing. Rule with me, and it will be good all round.'

## Be my priest (verse 4)

Now the honoured role of priest is introduced, with an oath of affirmation. The role of priest was vital to the practice of religious ceremony. So the king has religious as well as political and military responsibility. The priest bridged the gap between God and the people by obtaining forgiveness for the people, through the offering of sacrifices. The priest's own standing before God was vital. So, as priest, it is important that the king mirrored God's universal reign as king over heaven and earth. (See Psalm 72:1, 'Endow the king with your justice, O God, the royal son with your righteousness'.)

There are two further clues here about the nature of the royal priesthood. First, it is established 'for ever' and, secondly, it is like (or in true succession of) the priesthood of 'Melchizedek'. 'For ever' speaks both of security and duration, and it could not apply to the individual kings of Judah. It was understood to refer to the eternal significance of David's line, through which the Messiah would come. 'Melchizedek' is a name which is formed from two separate Hebrew words meaning 'king' and 'righteousness'. Melchizedek fulfilled the twin roles of priest and king (Genesis 14:18), and he stands as the example of how the king of Judah is also to fulfil both roles.

The writer of the Hebrews drew upon the example of Melchizedek to explain Jesus' exalted role as king and high priest for ever (Hebrews 5:1–10). 'Be my priest', the Lord is saying – but the requirements of this priesthood make it clear that no ordinary human king would ever be able to meet the ideals necessary.

## Trust me (verses 5–7)

The final three verses return to consider the military achievements of the king. The controlling idea is the phrase 'The Lord is at your right hand'. 'The Lord' may refer to the king, or to God himself. This phrase is a promise of safety and help which will lead to victory, justice and confidence. The language of these verses points forward to the establishment of God's kingdom and purposes through his chosen king. In relating this psalm to the life and ministry of Jesus, the New Testament writers declare that Jesus is the king through whom God works out his purposes. God's purposes will stand for ever, because Jesus is king and priest for ever – providing both rule and forgiveness.

## Questions

1. How might this psalm influence our attitudes when we are appointed to positions of leadership?
2. Scan through Hebrews 4:14 – 8:13. What can we learn about the person and work of Christ from these chapters? Do they tie up with the description of God's king-priest described in Psalm 110?
3. What difference does Christ's kingship and priesthood make to the world at large? What evidence is there of his rule?

# Psalm 111

## Hallelujah! Praise the Lord!

---

**The Lord has done much that merits our praise. All he does shows that he is completely devoted to his people.**

---

Are you in the mood for praising the Lord today? If not, read this psalm! If you are, join in with this song of praise!

This is the first of a series of three psalms which begins with 'Hallelu Yah', which means 'Praise the Lord'. The psalm itself illustrates why the Lord should be praised. Each line begins with a successive letter of the Hebrew alphabet. This arrangement, known as an acrostic, would have aided the process of memorizing the psalm, suggesting that the psalmist considered his work to contain truth well worth remembering! The psalm describes the character and action of God, and refers throughout to 'his people'. God is committed to his people. We need to hear that and hold on to it, because it is as certain as the fact that God is God.

In style and content the psalm is linked to the one which follows it: Psalm 111 is the theological basis for the understanding of human life and experience which is described in Psalm 112.

The first verse sets the mood for the whole psalm. You can feel a sense of joy: nothing can hold the writer back – he's in the business of praising God in the company of others who have experienced God's goodness.

### Hallelujah – you will always love us!

'The LORD is gracious and compassionate' (verse 4). This declaration of God's character sums up the reasons for praise given in verses 2–6. God's devotion to his people is shown by important events in Israel's history: the wonderful deliverance from slavery, the provision of food in the desert wanderings, and the establishment of the people in the land of their own. So the psalmist is basing his commitment to praise on his experience of the Lord's practical love for his people.

There are two reasons why the psalmist is confident in the love of God. He has seen it demonstrated in the past (verses 2–6), and its reality, based in covenant commitment, is known in the present (verses 7–9). The Lord has made a promise, a treaty with his people, which is set up with consequences which last 'for ever and ever' (verse 8). Nothing can undo this relationship, because it is tied up with the trustworthiness of the Lord himself.

## Hallelujah – praise you, Lord!

The final verse of the psalm emphasizes again God's right to receive praise because he brings understanding. The verse reminds us of many other Old Testament verses about the fear of the Lord (e.g. Proverbs 9:10). All these verses suggest that giving God his deserved respect is the way to experience life in its fullness and is therefore what true wisdom is all about. A noteworthy parallel is Psalm 86:11–12, which connects the fear of the Lord with having 'an undivided heart'. It is because the psalmist praises God with all his heart (verse 1) that he can give witness to the character of God and speak about wisdom in this way. It is this final verse which provides the link with the opening of Psalm 112.

## Questions

1. Try writing a psalm like this one. Be specific about what God has done in your life, in your housegroup, in your church. Then praise God through your own 'song of praise'.
2. What is the importance of reflecting on God's work in our lives? Do we give sufficient opportunity in our churches for people to speak out God's praise?
3. If someone totally ignorant of Christianity reads this psalm and no other part of the Bible, would it be sufficient to point the way to God's kingdom? If not, what is missing?

### Wisdom

Psalms 111 and 112 explain wisdom in terms of fearing the Lord. In the Old Testament, human wisdom is a quality which includes discernment, skill and knowledge. Wisdom is expressed by revering the Lord, who is the source of wisdom. So 'the fear of the Lord' is the appropriate response of awe and respect which results from contemplating the activity and nature of God. The psalmist confirms that he accepts that this is the only way to achieve security and blessing in this life. The same principle dominates the so-called wisdom literature of the Old Testament, especially Proverbs and Ecclesiastes.

## Psalm 112

## Hallelujah! Praise the Lord again!

**The Lord rewards those who devote their lives to him. This is a reason for praise.**

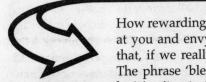

How rewarding is your life? Do people look at you and envy you? This psalm suggests that, if we really 'fear the Lord', they will. The phrase 'blessed is' could be translated 'how rewarding is the life of' or 'to be envied is the life of'. This might sound too good to be true – or you may feel that no-one else would want a life like yours – but this psalm suggests a rather different measure of happiness from that which we might normally use. The psalm says that a person who fears the Lord will experience darkness (verse 4), hear bad news (verse 7), and have opponents (verse 8), but somehow light, security and triumph will be known even in these difficult experiences.

This is the second of the series of psalms which begins 'Hallelu Yah' and, like Psalm 111, its content is arranged around successive letters of the Hebrew alphabet. 'His righteousness endures for ever' occurs once in Psalm 111 (about God himself) and twice in Psalm 112 (about the person who fears the Lord); the person who fears the Lord somehow participates in God's own eternal qualities. The final verse of Psalm 111 and the first verse of Psalm 112 are united in emphasizing 'the fear of the LORD'.

## Blessing is announced, described and missed

The Lord deserves praise because he is good to those who are devoted to him. Devotion expresses itself through an attitude of the heart (fear, reverence, honour) which is worked out in practice ('delight' in God's commands, verse 1, involves knowing them and simply loving to fulfil them). Here blessing is understood by the psalmist as God's gracious work which results in the recipient's good, both physically and spiritually. This is a reminder that God's people can never be proud of their own achievements nor self-satisfied with their circumstances: the benefits of God's blessing are limitless. There is always something more available in God's rich store of blessings!

The person who is devoted to the Lord will do the work that God does (verses 2–9). The result is that such a person can be described in terms which equally describe the character of God: 'upright', 'gracious' 'compassionate', 'righteous' (verse 4). I find this idea quite amazing and challenging. It suggests that, as my devotion to God is exercised, I will become recognizably 'like him'. Christ himself perfectly demonstrated such devotion and oneness with the character of his Father. This led to the centurion's unqualified recognition, 'Surely this was a righteous man' (Luke 23:47).

A further description of what blessing means comes in verse 8. The heart's security, a person's steadfastness and 'non-shakability', is dependent on God, not self. Someone who has no fear of bad news is not trusting in their own strength but trusting in God (verse 7). These two can become confused in everyday life, but God-dependency alone is reliable!

Those who oppose the righteous work of God miss out on the blessing. This is the unmistakable message of verse 10 and the inevitable conclusion of the psalm as a whole. Such people will be confused, destroyed and disappointed. The reality is that God has established a world on the principle of justice, and people receive the consequences of their actions. People who are not devoted to God do not recognize this fact and will always be vexed. There is a real warning to us all here: it is completely futile to turn our backs on God and his ways.

## Questions

1. What has this psalm to say to you about how you feel about your life at the moment?
2. Do our lives show 'God-likeness'? How far are we becoming less or more like Jesus? And how does this apply to our church?
3. Is there any evidence that Christians live a more 'blessed' life (materially and spiritually) than others? If so, why do people not always see it?

## Righteousness

Psalm 112 repeats that the person who fears God has enduring righteousness (verses 3 and 9). In the Bible, human right-eousness is not just about being right or doing right things, it includes relationship with God and being judged by God's own standards. Righteousness in God's sight can only be achieved through faith in Christ which enables relationship with God to be sustained (Romans 3:21–24). For this reason, someone who fears the Lord has righteousness which endures for ever, because their relationship with God endures. Righteousness is a work of God which has practical consequences in the lives of God-centred people.

# Psalm 113

## Hallelujah! Praise him yet again!

**The Lord of all is Lord for me. His people are compelled to praise him.**

This psalm is essentially about the Lord's transforming intervention in human lives. It is not surprising therefore that this last psalm in the Hallelujah triad is the first of a further set (113–118) known as the 'Egyptian Hallel'. This set of psalms is used at the Jewish festivals of Passover, Weeks, Tabernacles, Dedication and New Moon. These festivals are a celebration of God's saving intervention in his people's lives, so it is not surprising that the psalms are full of reference to historical events which give rise to unreserved praise. (Jesus would have almost certainly used Psalm 113 with his disciples during the Last Supper preceding his crucifixion – the ultimate demonstration of God's transforming intervention in human life.)

There are two other Hallel collections – the 'Great Hallel' (which includes Psalm 136), and the collection found at the end of the book (Psalms 146–150). All these sections take the praise of God as their over-riding theme – hence the repeated words 'Praise the Lord' or 'Hallelu Yah'.

Is God *too* great for you? In human relationships we often hear words like 'He's too good for me' or 'She's far above me', but this psalm asserts that the Lord is great, unique and above all, but that he is not *too* great for us. He is great, unique and above all *for the sake of* you and me. Such an idea is beyond our understanding of how relationships work out, but the psalmist has no hesitation in declaring it.

A striking feature of this psalm is its contrasts. God's praise is declared by individuals but known universally; God is enthroned in heaven but condescends to earth; God intervenes in particular lives but the results infiltrate the nations. All this amounts to what we might call 'the theology of good fortunes' but perhaps 'the theology of the reversal of fortunes' is less open to misinterpretation! The Lord turns things completely around. He challenges our view of himself and our view of ourselves – his timely and longed for interventions compel us to praise him and his ways.

## Praise the Lord's name

The object of praise is identified three times as 'the name of the LORD'. God made himself known to his people by his name, an indication that he wanted an intimate relationship with them. The Lord's people praise his name because the name represents to them something of what they know about their God and therefore they take delight in that name. We are encouraged to praise him, not blindly but out of our experience of his revealed nature. We can't escape the fact that there is something about the Lord. Verses 4–6 home in upon his uniqueness, kingly renown and authority. But these verses combine grandeur and condescension – graciously the Lord of all 'stoops down'.

Throughout his people's history the Lord has shown concern for individuals in the complete reversal of their fortunes. Barrenness was considered a curse from God, whereas children were a blessing (verses 7–9; see 1 Samuel 2, especially verse 8). The poor and needy lacked honour and dignity. The Lord is not satisfied with merely observing the plight of the unfortunate – he intervenes. These specific interventions gave rise to universal praise, for they mark strategic turning-points in the history of his people. We might think of the barrenness of Sarah and Rebekah and Rachel, or the rise of David from obscurity. The results of God's intervention reshaped the future of the people of Israel. So it was appropriate to sing songs like this one at the annual community festivals.

## Questions

---

1. In what ways are you a 'servant' of the Lord? How does this status affect your praise of the Lord?

2. What attitude do you have to those rejected as worthless in today's world? How does your attitude compare with the Lord's?

3. Is there anything we can do as servants of the Lord to see that the 'Lord is exalted over all the nations' (verse 4)?

### The name of the LORD

The 'name of the LORD' refers to all that goes to make up his character (see Exodus 3:13–14). The New Testament also speaks of 'the name' of the Lord (John 14:13–14; 17:11–12; Acts 3:6; Revelation 3:12). The followers of Jesus were given the name of Christ – Christians (literally meaning 'little Christs', Acts 11:25). Although it was used first as a term of ridicule, it came to mean that they were to be so identified with Jesus that their lifestyle would cause others to recognize that they belonged to him.

# Psalm 114

## Shake in your shoes!

**We, and all creation, should be overawed when we see God at work.**

When were you last completely overwhelmed by a sense of God's presence and power? Recently I was at a large evangelical gathering, praying with individuals who wanted to commit themselves more fully to the Lord's work. As we prayed, it was evident that God was present and working to bring renewal. It was wonderful and terrifying all at once, and I physically trembled with a sense of gratitude and joy. Even as I look back at the event, those feelings are still there. I think the psalmist would identify with my feelings. As he relates the story of the exodus – a story which would be very familiar to him – he celebrates with renewed amazement the wonder of God's presence and power.

This psalm was used at annual festivals to concentrate the people's minds on the history of their relationship with God, which was the inspiration for their present devotion to him. It is an invitation to remember afresh, to rekindle, even to nurture, those feelings of wonder which had inspired and motivated the Israelites who had experienced the miracles of the exodus at first hand.

The exodus experience included physical release from captivity (verse 1); safe passage to the promised land (verses 3–5 allude to the parting of the Red, or Reed, Sea and the Jordan); provision in the wilderness (verse 8 mentions the life-giving gift of water); and the eventual security of a homeland (verse 2). These events are significant, for they demonstrate the co-operation of the physical world with the purposes of God. Such co-operation involves the recognition of God's presence and power. (It is interesting to note that Joshua suggests that the purpose of the dividing of the Red Sea and the Jordan was 'so that all the peoples of earth might know that the hand of the LORD is powerful and so that you might always fear the LORD your God' (Joshua 4:20–24). Here the connection is made between the events of the exodus, the recognition of the Lord's power, and the response of fear and reverence from his people. This is exactly the theme of the psalm.)

So this psalm asks us, along with the physical world, to respond appropriately to God's presence and power. God's presence always demands a response from us – that's why Jesus' life produced such sharp divisions among those who met him. Ultimately, however, all creation must co-operate with God's demonstration of power, for all he had made is at his disposal as the events of the exodus remind us.

## Questions

1. This psalm reminds us not to be complacent about knowing the reality of God's presence for ourselves. What things could help us as we ask God to make us more aware of his presence in our lives, our churches and our world?
2. What do the events of the exodus teach us about the nature of God's work?
3. How far do you think that the history of the Jewish people in the twentieth century, and the establishment of the Israeli state, are part of God's plan, as was the exodus from Egypt?

# Psalm 115

## God does whatever pleases him

**Whatever challenges you face, trust in God, since he is the true source of all help.**

This psalm highlights the folly of idol worship, proclaims the certainty of the Lord's sovereign control, and summons us to trust him and praise him for ever. It seems  likely that it was originally used as a liturgical reading, because it contains distinct sections of prayer, assurance and blessing which various members of the worshipping community could have spoken to each other for mutual encouragement.

How can we face today and tomorrow? The struggle of faith requires us to play our part, but it is the certainty of God's work for us which will secure the triumph of our faith. In fact this is the emphasis in this psalm: God loves, acts, helps and blesses. So it is obvious why this psalm was used at the annual festivals:

it celebrates God's intervention in his people's lives and ends with the resounding invitation, 'Praise the LORD'.

### We praise our God

Praise dominates the psalm – it is there at the beginning and the end. In the Hebrew text there is no 'and' between 'love' and 'faithfulness' (verse 1). They are characteristics of God which are very closely linked. God's people are the benefactors of his love-and-faithfulness so his people must praise him. This is indeed the message of verses 16–18: 'it is we who extol the LORD'. There is another parallel between the opening verse and the concluding verses. Both contain a negative statement followed by a positive one, underlining who should be praised and who should do the praising. It is this which makes best sense of verse 16. It does not imply that God is not in control on the earth (that would deny the central message of the psalm), but it gives a reason for praise: God has given the earth to those who live on it so that we can praise him now and for ever (verse 18).

### We trust our God

In verses 2–11 a clear contrast is made between the gods of the nations and the Lord of Israel. Israel trusts the Lord who is her help, and shield, whereas the nations trust idols who cannot do anything for them because they originate with human hands (verse 4). (There is great irony here, because the idols are less able than the people who have made them who can speak, see, hear, smell and feel.) In contrast God is enthroned in heaven and 'does whatever he pleases' (verse 3). In fact the whole of the second half of this psalm celebrates that the Lord is pleased to work for our good. It is consequently as foolish not to trust the Lord as it is foolish to trust idols, emphasized by the threefold repetition in verses 9–11 of 'trust in the LORD'.

### Our God blesses us

The psalm ends with a crescendo of praise celebrating God's presence. He shows us himself by giving both spiritual and material benefits. It is interesting that God's work of blessing is connected to his role as 'Maker of heaven and earth' (verse 15), for this means that the way God blesses us is consistent with who he has made us to be. Sometimes we need reminding that, when it comes to blessing us, God knows best! It is because God chooses to bless his people that they will praise him and trust him, for his relationship and his presence with them is established. This relationship with God enables God's people to stand firm in testing times.

## Questions

1. Why do we find it difficult to praise God sometimes? How does this psalm help us?
2. By using this psalm corporately, God's people are able to encourage each other in their faith. How important is this? How can we follow this example in our churches today?
3. What forms of idolatry exist in our world today? What other gods are worshipped? What attitude should we adopt to those who have not put their trust in the Lord?

# Psalms 116–117

## The Lord saved me, Hallelujah!

**If you love the Lord and have experienced his goodness, tell everyone about it and praise him.**

### I was in trouble (Psalm 116)

What do you feel like doing when you experience the wonder and joy of answered prayer? Perhaps you fall on your knees in silent adoration. Perhaps you get on the telephone and tell everyone about it.

Perhaps you jump up and down with excitement and can't stop rejoicing. Perhaps you are moved to prayers of worship or dedication.

As you read through this psalm, you can detect each of the feelings which underlie these responses. The psalmist recalls his experience of answered prayer. His prayer is summarized in the brief statement, 'O LORD, save me!' (verse 4) and the testimony to God's response is the unreserved proclamation 'he saved me' (verse 6). The psalm declares God's goodness alongside the trouble which the psalmist experienced. The result is words of devotion and finally of praise. The psalm jumps around from one of these themes to another, just as answered prayer sometimes brings a mixture of thoughts and feelings all at once, as an amazing sense of relief overcomes us.

We do not know the exact circumstances which troubled the psalmist, but obviously the situation was dire. The trouble is likened to the pain and despair of death in verse 3, and verse 10 implies that the psalmist could see no way out of his trouble. Verse 11 may mean that human help had failed. No wonder the person so anguished would be 'overcome by trouble and sorrow' (verse 3). In verse 16 the image of chains is used, suggesting that this trouble felt like permanent imprisonment. It is noteworthy that there is no complaint that this dire trouble had been experienced – just thankfulness for God's intervention.

## The Lord heard my cry

This song of praise begins with this announcement of truth. Praise and love and thanks are offered to God because he has chosen to listen to one particular cry for help. Our prayers can make a difference. This is guaranteed by God's character and love for his people which moves him to act for their good (verses 5–6). It is he who protects, saves and frees. He protects his people who face death-like situations because their lives are precious to him (verse 15). It is almost as if the psalmist is suggesting that God's saving work was inevitable because God is who he is.

The psalm starts with a blunt statement of devotion and

affection, 'I love the LORD'. It is the obvious response to the Lord's act of salvation and it requires practical outworking. The psalmist commits himself to show his love for the Lord by continuing to call on him (verses 2, 13, 17), by living in recognition of the Lord's presence (verse 9), by being the Lord's servant (verse 16), by fulfilling his vows (verses 14, 18), and by acts of worship (verses 13, 17). In fact 'the cup of salvation' may simply refer to part of the thankoffering which became a symbol of the Lord's deliverance of his people. This was taken up in the celebration of the Passover when the psalm was used to express thanks for the exodus. This psalm is also used by Christians in the celebration of the Lord's Supper, where the cup is a symbol of thanksgiving for the act of salvation by Jesus on the cross. Surely our response to such salvation can be expressed by the psalmist's own choice of words 'I love the LORD' – a testimony in itself to the Lord's goodness and an invitation to all his people to join and praise him.

## Praise the Lord, everybody! (Psalm 117)

Psalm 117, the shortest of all the psalms, is a brief hymn which takes the praise of the Lord as its theme. Despite its brevity it is significant, for it calls all nations, all peoples to praise the Lord. There is no special focus on the people of Israel and this psalm seems to anticipate the time when all people will worship the Lord (an idea prominent in some prophetic passages, e.g. Isaiah 66:23; it is taken up in the New Testament, see Romans 15:11, not least in connection with the universal worship of Jesus, see Philippians 2:9–11).

The reason given for praising the Lord is also of interest. Because God upholds the universe, all people experience his loving commitment to them. Certainly the psalm suggests that the praise of God is always incomplete when all his creation is not involved in it. This speaks to me of the ultimate value of all human beings as people, and above all, as worshipping people.

## Questions

1. Do we place value on personal testimony to God's goodness in our corporate acts of worship together? What do you like or dislike about this?
2. Do you feel you have to put on an act when you come to worship God with others? What does this psalm teach us about the relationship between public worship and our private experiences of God?
3. What does Psalm 116 suggest about making and keeping of vows and promises made to God?

# Psalm 118

## The Lord has become my salvation

**The Lord helps us when we are in great need. So let's join with others in celebrating his love and giving him our thankful praise.**

 This psalm has a great deal in common with Psalm 116. It jumps around from praise to despair rather unexpectedly and, like Psalm 116, it has been prompted by a particular victory which leads the author to give thanks and praise. It is the final psalm in the Hallel set (used at annual festivals) which began with Psalm 113.

The structure of the psalm seems to require different readers at different points – hence the move from singular to plural indicates the move from the main speaker (probably the king or a representative of the people) to the gathered congregation. This liturgy may have been connected originally to a procession (see verse 27). This is probably why the crowds in Jesus' lifetime used the words of verse 26 when Jesus entered Jerusalem (see Matthew 21:9; Mark 11:9; Luke 19:38; John 12:13).

By this time the psalm would have been recognized as looking forward to the Messiah (note the expressions 'I will not die but live', verse 17; and the rejected capstone image, verse 22, which was taken up in 1 Peter 2:7). These connections with Jesus' life and ministry are particularly interesting because the name 'the LORD' (Yahweh) appears in almost every verse. This reminds us of God's close presence with his people, which was shown supremely in the life of Jesus himself – the person who 'comes in the name of the LORD' (verse 26; compare Matthew 21:9) to bring God's salvation. The whole psalm rejoices in the fact that God's love means he works for our salvation; this idea is clearly demonstrated in verse 21, where salvation is the specific reason for giving thanks to God.

## I was in trouble but the Lord saved me

Verses 5–21 combine the reality of dire circumstances with the realization that the Lord saves. Human strength crumbles in the presence of God; what can human beings do (verse 6) when God's right hand is at work (verses 15–16)? Ultimate faith is expressed and such faith is based on the experience of salvation. The result is that praise can't be held back – it's absolutely bursting out from the saved person (verses 14–16, 19, 21) and those he represents (verses 26–27).

'O LORD, save us' (verse 25) is the one-word prayer 'Hosanna' in the Hebrew language. This is both a recognition that the Lord can save and a request that he will do so. In making this prayer, the people recognize their need of the Lord's intervention in their lives and invite him to show the reality of his presence. So this corporate prayer is a suitable climax to this psalm, leading as it does to the theological statement 'the LORD is God' (verse 27). This may sound obvious, but it assumes a particular meaning when applied prophetically to Jesus implying 'the Lord [Jesus] is God'.

## Questions

1. How does this psalm help us to understand what was going on when Jesus entered Jerusalem to the crowds' shouts of 'Hosanna'? Read Matthew 21:1–17. Why would the teachers of the law be 'indignant'?
2. What is the importance and meaning of verse 22? (See 1 Peter 2, and see *The capstone* below.)
3. In this psalm the main speaker encourages the gathered people to give thanks to God. What is your attitude when you join in with praise, either in responsive spoken words or in song? Do you have a duty to contribute to times of praise in your church?

### The capstone

A 'capstone' (verse 22) or 'cornerstone' is a term used for an important stone in a building's design. It is a term which could be used for a stone at the top or bottom of a building, but is always used of a vital stone which gives a building its strength and stability. It could therefore be used of a stone which completes and supports an arch-like structure, or a foundation corner stone which would hold together rows of stones. Such stones are essential, and are understood to be the glory of a building's design. In Old Testament prophetic literature, the term is used for a human figure who will bring stability, justice and salvation (see Isaiah 28:16; Zechariah 10:4). It is this use which is assumed in the New Testament where Jesus' role in the church as her foundation and glory is explored (see 1 Peter 2:6–7; also Matthew 22:42; Mark 12:10; Luke 20:17; Acts 4:10–11). Thus, when Jesus is rejected by unbelievers, they stumble and fall like a building without foundations (Romans 9:33).

# Psalm 119

## I delight in your law

**God's words reflect his good and loving character. It is worth dedicating our lives to learning about, living out and making known his commands.**

Have you ever tried your hand at writing poetry? Sometimes a poem can be written without much planning and forethought as the ideas just seem to flow from the pen as we express feelings, philosophies or descriptions. At other times poems may be the result of a great deal of planning and ordering; sometimes the very structure and progression of the poem underlines the message we are seeking to convey.

This psalm is not a spontaneous song but a rather ornate and highly structured piece of writing. Like some of the previous psalms we have looked at, its content is organized around the twenty-two successive letters of the Hebrew alphabet, but this time there is a set of eight lines for each letter – hence the psalm's overall length of 176 verses! The use of successive letters of the alphabet was a device used to aid memory.

The psalm is basically a declaration of trust, and of devotion to God and his law. It ends with the writer's prayer that God will bless him as he continues to live in the light of God's Word and thereby bring God his praise. A series of words is used to refer to God's Word: 'law' (or 'Torah', see p. 154), 'precepts', 'commands', 'decrees', 'word' and 'promise'. Though each term has its own particular emphasis, together they serve to stress God's enduring and authoritative teaching.

The psalm links the character of God with the nature of his word. The psalmist has discovered the nature of God through the study of his law. He understands God's word to be his direct communication to his people and that is what gives it its value. So this psalm describes the collected words of God as awesome, eternal, just, faithful and true. In other words they are like God himself and they exist for our good.

## Rejoice in God's law!

Have you ever thought of God as a bit of a spoil-sport? Have you ever sympathized with non-Christians when they express their view that Christianity is all about keeping a set of miserable commandments? No such negativism is even entertained in this psalm. The attitude to God's law is all positive as the psalmist confirms his long-standing devotion to God's word. Attitudes such as these are littered throughout the psalm:

- I willingly live by God's law
- I want to study and learn more about God's law
- I will talk about the law – all the time, to all people
- I really want other people to love the law too
- I pin all my hopes on God's law
- I jump for joy because of the law.

The psalmist has come to realize that life with God's law at the centre is life with God (verse 151), and that can only be a cause for rejoicing.

## The benefits of the law

Repeatedly the psalmist stresses that being devoted to the law of God has worked only for his good. The knowledge of God's law brings light, life, wisdom, salvation, pleasure, delight, comfort and direction. It enables sin to be resisted (verses 9–11) and pressure to be overcome (verses 50–52). In his own words 'the law from your mouth is more precious to me than thousands of pieces of silver and gold' (verse 72). The psalmist never praises the law itself – it is the Lord (from whom the law originates) who deserves our praise and worship. The same point is made in verse 57: it is the Lord who is the psalmist's portion. It is relationship with the Lord which the psalmist seeks, through examining the law. He strives to know God's salvation (verses 166, 174), and the aim of his life is to praise God (verse 175).

## Questions

1. When did you last feel negative about God's laws? Do you often feel like this? How does this psalm challenge you to change your attitudes?
2. Is there a place for keeping rules in the church? How can we tell the difference between legalism and a positive attitude to God's law? (Romans 8 and Galatians 3 are important passages on this subject.)
3. Does God's law apply to all people, even though they have never read any of it? How can they know what it is? (Look at Romans 1.)

## Torah

The Hebrew word 'Torah' means 'teaching, instruction, direction'. It is especially used of the first five books of the Bible, the 'Pentateuch', but it is also applied to the whole Old Testament as a source for God's revealed direction and teaching. It is not a word which implies negative restrictions, which our word 'law' sometimes implies, because it provides the possibility of life lived to the full. Torah is an inclusive word meaning all the direction and guidance which God gives. It is God's gift for the good of his people (see, e.g. Deuteronomy 4:40; 5:33), and they are called to respond to it in love and obedience (Deuteronomy 6:24–25). Torah, then, does not deny the reality of God's grace but is an important expression of it being concerned with enjoying life as God intended it to be. Jesus' own attitude to the Torah reminds us that its purpose was to promote and preserve relationship to God and each other.

Jesus shows this by highlighting the two great commands of the Torah: love God, and love one another (Matthew 22:37–40).

# Psalm 120

## Peace where there is no peace

**Even peace-loving people can be treated with hostility – but the Lord will rescue them.**

Do you think of yourself as a 'person of peace'? Do you long for harmony between people and between people and God? The psalmist sees himself like this (verse 7), but his problem is that people around him stand for the complete opposite (verse 6). In fact, they love lies and deceit, and we know all too well in family, church, social and spiritual life (i.e. relationship with God), that there is never peace, wholeness and harmony when lies and deceit are present.

The theme of peace links the set of Psalms 120–134, which are known as the 'songs of ascents' (cf. p. 27). Some of them concentrate on how knowing the Lord's presence and mercy brings peace (see Psalms 121, 123, 124, 126, 127, 130, 131 and 132). Others contain prayers for peace and unity (see Psalms 122:6–9; 125:5; 128:5–6; 133:1), and we also find prayers for blessing which incorporate the desire for peace (see, e.g. 128:5; 129:8; 134:3).

It appears that Psalm 120 was originally a prayer of an individual which assumed new meaning for the community in a hostile environment. The set of Psalms 120–134 was probably used by pilgrims (the title 'songs of ascents' refers to going up the temple hill) because they recall the promise of the Lord's presence with his people.

## The Lord will save the peace-loving person

Verses 1 and 2 contain the psalmist's request, 'Save me', and identify the root of his problem. He is in distress because of the lies and deceit which other people have used against him. It is obvious from verses 5–7 that he feels hemmed in on every side by people who only intend him harm because they love hostility. (The references to 'Meshech' and 'the tents of Kedar', two places quite distant from each other, suggest that the psalmist feels hated by everyone. Alternatively, these places might be mentioned because they were known centres of hostility.) When human hostility is as real as this, there is no alternative but to trust the Lord for deliverance. In calling himself a person of peace, the psalmist is confirming his co-operation with God's own purposes. This is the basis of his confidence and the foundation of the prayer 'Save me'.

## The Lord will punish the haters of peace

The psalmist believes God will vindicate him through punishing those who practise lies and deceit. The tongue is often portrayed as a deadly weapon with potential for harm (see Psalms 57:4; 64:3; Jeremiah 9:3, 8). Verse 4 emphasizes that the punishment of the liars fits their crime. The broom tree was a good source of fuel, and so it is a powerful image of effective punishment (cf. the association between burning coal and divine punishment in Psalms 11:6; 140:9–10). The psalmist is therefore expressing his confidence that the Lord will punish his opponents severely and appropriately.

This psalm announces clearly that peace and salvation are the rewards of those who seek peace, whatever the circumstances may suggest. In contrast, liars and deceivers will experience God's just punishment.

## Questions

1. In what ways do liars sometimes appear to have the upper hand in your experience? How does this make you feel? Can

you feel with the psalmist in his distress?

2. How can we cultivate peace in hostile situations? Why might we want to do this? Think of examples in your church.
3. Are we ever tempted to lie or deceive? What motivates these temptations?
4. What has this psalm to say to us when we want to mete out our own punishments on those who are hostile to us? Is there a place for 'vigilantes' to police a threatened neighbourhood? If not, and if the police are not able to help, do we leave our security to God?

# Psalms 121–122

## Where can I get help?

**The Lord is always ready to help. Jerusalem is the symbol of his presence and safety.**

### My help comes from the Lord (Psalm 121)

The second pilgrim psalm pictures life as a journey with the Lord in which we exercise trust and experience his care. God is our guardian or keeper, watching over us to protect and provide for us. The psalm's key is the confident assertion of verse 2, which is the response to 'Where can I get help'? The help which the Lord offers is appropriate, timely, dependable and durable. The best way to find help from this psalm is to keep reading it – perhaps even memorize it – and then recall its words at the start of each day as a reminder of the Lord's presence and care.

The first two verses are the psalmist's personal testimony that God is the source of his help. Describing the Lord as 'the Maker of heaven and earth' establishes the reliability of God's help.

The phrase 'I lift up my eyes to the hills' may be a recognition that people look to the hill-top shrines of other gods for help, but it could mean looking up and around in general. Verse 2 is therefore the confident solution of the search: help comes not from hills or shrines, but from the Lord.

The remainder of the psalm focuses on how the Lord watches over the psalmist's life. This selection of promises, given in response to his words of faith and trust, could have been spoken by a priest in the context of worship. (There are certainly parallels with the priestly blessing in Numbers 6:24–26, e.g. the idea of the Lord 'keeping/watching' and the result of 'peace', a key theme in these pilgrim psalms.)

The first promise (verse 3) implies safe walking in the journey of life. God does not take his eye off us; he doesn't sleep. This guarantee has implications for our protection in varied circumstances, whether danger from opponents ('shade at your right hand' may refer to someone who stands with you to offer protection in the face of opposition), or from natural elements (the moon and sun were seen as threats to physical well-being). The non-sleeping Lord is a shade and cover. Verses 7–8 emphasize the scope and duration of God's protection: all life's journeys are for ever under the Lord's watchful gaze.

This psalm does not promise that we will know no unpleasant times on the journey of life, but rather it rejoices that we live under the umbrella of God's protective guard, and we can be confident of his help.

## Fullness of joy (Psalm 122)

The pilgrims reach Jerusalem. They praise the Lord for the city and then pray for blessing on it. Their praise, however, is reserved for God, not the city. This is confirmed by the reference to Jerusalem as 'the house of the LORD' in the first and last verses of the psalm. It is the presence of God which gives Jerusalem her special status. This point is equally true of the psalms known as the 'Songs of Zion' (see Psalms 46 and 48), which often begin with the praise of God himself. Jerusalem is the place where God's people praise him (verse 4) and it is associated with rejoicing (verse 1). It is also a place of security and unity, for it holds together (verse 3). It stands for decisions of justice (verse 5) and therefore reflects the character of God himself. For these characteristics the Lord is to be praised because his presence is the controlling influence.

Verses 6–9 express the longing that peace may be found in the city of God. Peace is ultimately about enjoying the presence of God. It is the gift of God which comes particularly from being accepted by him and being able to live in his presence. Security and justice are further aspects of God's peace, and verses 6 and 7 call upon God to exercise his justice. Two reasons are given for the prayer for peace: that the pilgrim's friends would benefit (verse 8), and that the honour of God's house would be upheld (verse 9). So the request for peace is for the sake of the whole worshipping community and for the honour of God. The psalm is a celebration, based on faith in the benefits of God's presence and the enduring honour of God's name.

## Questions

1. Why do you enjoy (or not enjoy) going to church?
2. Do we pray in ways which aim to bring benefits to others and honour to God? What kinds of prayer achieve this?
3. It is fashionable to 'look to the hills' today in forms of nature-worship, paganism, New Age worship and so on. How can we guide such worshippers to the truth?

# Psalms 123–124

## Have mercy on us, Lord

---

**When in trouble we can turn to God for he is on our side.**

---

### Looking to God (Psalm 123)

It is fitting that this psalm, following one about entering God's presence, reflects on the need for mercy. It also reminds us that God's people experience changes of circumstances which do not mean that their trust in God need waver. The psalm encourages us to turn to the Lord for help (as did Psalm 121), just as a servant might look to the person he or she serves for favour or relief.

The purpose of the prayer 'have mercy' is to move God to intervene. God's people are fed up and worn out by those who have shown them only ridicule and contempt. These attitudes show a lack of respect and total rejection, and it is therefore a prayer of great trust to ask the God 'whose throne is in heaven' (verse 1) to give mercy and favour. Such action on God's part would display his respect and acceptance to those who look to him for help. This prayer is a request to the Lord to reverse totally the fortunes of his people. The prayer is based on the confident words 'My help comes from the LORD' (Psalm 121:2).

### 'What if . . .' (Psalm 124)

Have you ever been in a near-death situation? I remember travelling in West Africa on crammed, dilapidated public transport when we were involved in an accident in which people might well have lost their lives. In fact, no-one was seriously hurt, and as we had just read Psalm 91 we were convinced that God's angels had something to do with it! Nonetheless a whole series of 'what ifs' crowded into our minds.

In this psalm God's people reflect on their troubled journey as his people and rejoice that the tragic 'what if' experience didn't happen, because the Lord intervened to save them. In many ways the psalm echoes the words of Romans 8:31, 'If God is for us, who can be against us?' The people's experiences confirm that they have nothing to fear from life's threats because God fights on their side. The title of this song of ascents associates it with the life of David; certainly David knew dangers comparable with those described by the imagery here.

Verses 2–7 describe the wide-ranging dangers which God's people faced. Nature in its entirety is implicated as the source of danger: the earth (the seat of human menace, verses 2–3), water (verses 4–5) and sky (verse 7) are mentioned (the accepted threefold division of nature). But the danger is resolved by deliverance (verse 8). The Lord's ability and right to overturn danger is asserted by his title 'the Maker of heaven and earth'. The Lord longs to help and is able to help, not least due to the reality of his presence in heaven and earth, implied by the references to his name (verse 8). This psalm reaffirms the Lord's special care for his people alongside acknowledging his universal sovereignty.

## Questions

1. Why do we need mercy from God? Why can't we cope on our own? How far is God's mercy channelled through other people? Be specific.
2. Which of the images in Psalm 124 most aptly describes danger which you have experienced? What things in life make you feel so afraid that you really do have to 'throw yourself on the Lord' and trust for his deliverance?
3. Why is it important to hold together God's universal sovereignty and his particular love for his people? How does this help us to make sense of life's circumstances?

# Psalm 125

## We are like Mount Zion

**God's people are as safe and secure as Mount Zion because they are protected by the Lord himself.**

As the pilgrim people look at Mount Zion, they are reminded that they are protected by the Lord because he surrounds them (verse 2) and enables them to stand firm for ever (verse 1). The psalm rejoices in God's protection. His people can know peace because the Lord encompasses them with his care. There are conditions to knowing God's protection, for the Lord's true people are those who trust him (verse 1) and are 'upright in heart' (verse 4). This phrase implies that the whole person must be set on pursuing that which is good in the eyes of God, and that involves undying loyalty to the Lord himself.

Verse 3 suggests that God will show his protection by removing evil from the land belonging to his people. The word 'sceptre' is used as a symbol of rule, implying that the ruling force of evil itself will be removed. Verse 3 could also mean that foreign domination will be removed (including the foreign religions which would accompany it). The removal of wickedness stops God's people from being tempted by evil and judged because of it. It is a way of ensuring that their peace, and their status as God's people, remains their reality.

## We are protected by the Lord's good hand

Confidence is expressed in verse 4. The people of God know he delights in their good, and so their request for God to 'do good' is based on their faith in him. But their request is also an expression of their commitment; it is the good and upright who can depend on God's own goodness. This confidence in the justice of God to deal with people appropriately is continued in verse 5; those who desert the way of goodness will be led away to punishment. God's goodness demands such justice for it is a way of protecting his faithful people.

In common with the other songs of ascents, this one too focuses on peace. The request for peace (verse 5) is based on the certain hope that the Lord's people will know peace because of the special status they have as the Lord's protected people. But there is no place for complacency. We are always required to show our dedication and loyalty to the Lord. Bringing peace is clearly the Lord's work, and so we must always live as his grateful people.

## Questions

1. What do you think of when you think of a mountain? Are these thoughts consistent with how you feel as a Christian, strong and immovable? If not, what is missing?
2. What lessons and warnings are there in this psalm for Christians today?
3. How do we answer the charge of arrogance if we claim that Christians are the Lord's protected people?

## Zion

G. A. F. Knight has some helpful information about the development and use of the term 'Zion' (verse 1). He writes,

> At the north-east corner of the city there was the highest point, known as Mount Zion. The significance of the word Zion grew and developed over the centuries:
> a) Zion was where the temple and royal palace stood, that is to say, on it was found the seat both of government and of divine worship.
> b) Later on, Zion became a poetic name for the people of Israel themselves.

c) Still later, after they were driven from Jerusalem in 587 BC by the Babylonian conquerors, Zion came to be used of the whole people of God.

d) Sometimes the name was even used for the little local church building which one attended Sunday after Sunday.

e) But in church liturgy Zion came to be used as the name even of the heavenly city!

(G. A. F. Knight, *Psalms*, vol. 1)

# Psalm 126

## The Lord can do it again

**When we face challenging circumstances, we can be confident that the Lord who has changed things in the past can do the same again.**

### What a dream!

Dreams can vary a lot in terms of their theme and the effects they have on us. But the common thing about dreams is that they don't feel like reality. We talk about dreams being 'too good to be true'. We warn those who expect too much out of life by saying 'Don't get carried away by your dreams' and such advice seems wise. But then, of course, we meet the exuberant friend jumping up and down telling everyone in earshot 'My dreams have come true!' The result is usually infectious joy and enthusiasm, maybe tinged by a hint of jealousy. Think of the young couple announcing their engagement or a planned pregnancy. Think of the longterm unemployed person getting a job, or the lottery addict winning the jackpot. Shared surprise, unbelief, pleasure – the result of a realized dream, however short-lived that dream might turn out to be.

The first three verses of this psalm are all about such feelings. When the Lord restored the fortunes of his people it felt like a dream come true. The clues given about this dream-like experience suggest that it was about the return of the people from exile to their homeland. It was a miracle of God's provision, and the reality of their new-found freedom didn't sink in easily. The outcome of this 'dream come true' was unbounded joy (verse 2) and unreserved praise to God himself (verses 2–3). God's praise was found on the lips of his rescued people and also those others who had witnessed the rescue ('the nations'). When God acts in miraculous ways, it is hardly surprising that everyone sits up and takes notice. When dreams come true in the lives of God's people, the only appropriate response is to thank the Lord himself.

### Dreams can be repeated

Verses 4–6 are a confident prayer that the dream-like experience might become reality all over again. 'If it happened once it can happen again'. The imagery used suggests that this possibility is tied up with the Lord's role as creator and restorer. In the patterns of nature, the Lord turns the dried-up Negev into streams of water and blesses the sower of seed through the sheaves of the harvest.

It seems as if God's people were facing renewed difficulty (perhaps the resettling of the returned people into their homeland) and so they reminded themselves that the Lord was capable of doing amazing things as he had showed in the past. The result is a clear anticipation of another dream-like experience, coupled with the anticipation of the joy which would accompany it. What an amazing thought! The dreams we experience as reality by God's good hand can be our repeated joy over and over again.

### Questions

1. Do you think of yourself as someone with your 'feet on the ground' all the time? Is there anything wrong with dreaming

about what God can do for you? Why might this be helpful/unhelpful to you?

2. In this psalm there is solemn recognition of God's greatness alongside unreserved joy. How can we find this balance in our own private and public worship?

3. Why did 'the nations' recognize God's greatness (verse 2)? What does this suggest about the way we expect the unbelieving world to respond to what God does?

## The Negev

The Negev was the desert region to the south of Judea. The name itself means 'dry' and was an appropriate name for this arid area. It was originally the land of the Amalekites but was handed over to the tribes of Judah and was the scene of many of David's exploits. The reference to 'the Negev' in this psalm reflects its reputation as a dry and arid place. The people needed blessing and hope in their new situation, just as flowing streams were needed in the desert.

# Psalm 127

## Life is worthless without the Lord

**All our human effort is futile unless the Lord helps us, provides for us and rewards us.**

Different psalms stick in your mind for different reasons. I have at least two good reasons for not being able to forget this psalm. First, it was the basis of the sermon at my wedding, and second it was read at the dedication service

following the birth of our first son. Certainly the words in verse 3 make it very appropriate to any service thanking God for the gift of children, and some have suggested that this may have been the original use of the psalm. In the course of ten years of marriage, I have often called to mind the rest of the psalm too – for it is really about not getting things out of perspective, but trusting God to intervene in our lives to make our efforts worthwhile. In practice this means two things: I should not judge the success or failures of my efforts by human standards, but I should always do my best, recognizing that all I have is a gift from God. Such a balance gives value to human effort while affirming dependence on our Lord.

Because the psalm is about human experience it is sometimes called a 'wisdom psalm' and this explains the link with Solomon in its title. It brings the secular and religious worlds together; what we believe about God will influence what we believe about life. Hence our activity and our worship will correspond to each other and the result will be blessing and peace.

### The Lord works in the routines of life

When this psalm was originally used, its particular themes and images carried immediate meaning. Building a house, keeping watch over cities, toiling for food, contending for family justice at the city gates, were mainstay occupations. Everyone knew about these tasks and their value was not disputed. The idea that these tasks could be 'in vain' or worthless was quite a shock, but the psalmist emphasizes that all life is worthless unless it is lived with the Lord. This was after all the experience of God's pilgrim people: they realized their need for the Lord's presence over and over again. These particular tasks of life were about home-making (verse 1), security (verse 1), working for income and food (verse 2), having a family (verses 3–5) and being treated with respect. We note that human aspirations have not changed much. For God's people, then and now, it is only as we recognize the Lord's hand in the routines of life that those routines, and our lives, have any value.

## Count your blessings

If we have children we should view them as precious gifts from the Lord. 'More easily said than done', we may well respond! But here children are described as being like 'arrows in the hands of a warrior', in other words, they will be ready to defend and protect you when there is trouble. In addition verse 5 speaks about contending 'in the gate', the place where judicial decisions would be made about family rights. Again the point is that children will try to protect the family and will contend for justice. By concluding here the psalm has turned full circle – like the builder and the watchman, the children work for the family's welfare. It is when family life is lived in the presence of God that such labours are fruitful and meaningful and peaceful, for the Lord gives sleep and rest to those he loves (verse 2).

## Questions

1. Do you find it difficult to sleep sometimes? What circumstances lead to this? How do we deal with a lack of sleep? How does it make us feel?
2. In what ways can we acknowledge God's presence and work in our family life?
3. Sometimes our children don't live up to the expectations of this psalm. Why might this be? What challenges does this psalm pose to children and parents?

## Watchmen

In Old Testament times watchmen were stationed on city walls and hill tops in order to warn the people of imminent attack. They played a vital role in defending a city and their responsibility was well respected. The reference to watchmen in this psalm makes it clear that their ability to defend a city was limited. Even if they played their part well, ultimate security lies in the hands of God.

## City gates

The gates of a city (verse 5) were the place where legal business was conducted and disputes were settled. Trade was also carried out here and important announcements were delivered especially in regard to matters of justice and punishment. The promise of verse 5 means that people who know the Lord's hand rewarding them will also benefit from just treatment at the hand of human dispensers of justice.

# Psalm 128

## Live for the Lord!

**We are encouraged to live our lives to please the Lord because this will be for our good.**

This psalm continues the theme of Psalm 127 by speaking of blessing in terms of its practical results in family life. But the vision here is wider, for personal blessing is extended into the experience of the worshipping community in verses 5–6. Whereas Psalm 127 focuses on the gift of children, the first four verses of Psalm 128 appear to centre on the blessing of a fruitful and loyal wife. Perhaps this psalm was used originally as a wedding song. Even so, with their mention of Zion, the last two verses contain sentiments familiar in the present collection of the songs of ascents.

## Joy in your home

We all crave more happiness in our daily life and that's exactly what verses 1–4 promise you if you live your life respecting the Lord and his commands. It's a big 'if' but it's a big promise! In verse 2 the joy comes from fruitful labour (bringing food, the basic necessity of life) and beyond that prosperity (that which is over and above our needs). The imagery of verse 3 conveys the sense of joy coupled with fulfilment which comes through the faithfulness of a wife and sons. A 'fruitful vine' is also a symbol of beauty, and 'olive shoots' symbolize strength. So the imagery is all about your highest hopes coming to fruition and the sense of security and pride which comes with such realized aspirations.

The final two verses identify the Lord himself as the source of blessing. This blessing includes the desire that the prosperity of Jerusalem will be witnessed. These words confirm the idea that the personal joy of verses 1–4 is tied up intimately with the fortunes of Jerusalem as the focal point of community life. Real joy and peace will always be *shared*, and for this reason the final words form a summary to the psalm as a whole: when the Lord is revered in Israel, blessing will come and peace will follow.

## Questions

1. Do we overlook the blessings we have in our lives? How can we correct such attitudes? Make practical proposals.
2. Why do you think this psalm was written?
3. How can we make sense of times when people who fear the Lord are not blessed in the ways this psalm suggests?

# Psalm 129

## We've been through so much

---

**We keep going because we can remember how the Lord has helped us in the past. Our confident prayer is that the Lord will continue to be victorious over his enemies.**

---

 Compare the beginning of this psalm with that of Psalm 124. Both begin with words which are repeated, suggesting that the leader of the gathered people invites them to join in by using the cue 'let Israel say'. This psalm reminds us that the pilgrim people have their experience of God to call on as they face the reality of life.

### Looking back

The people are aware that they have gone through testing times and yet they credit their survival to the loyalty of the Lord (verse 4). By declaring 'the LORD is righteous' they affirm that the Lord has upheld justice through his committed actions for the sake of his people. This does not, however, remove the pain and reality of their suffering. They have been 'greatly oppressed' (verses 1–2), which could imply the severity and the repeated nature of their suffering. The pain was felt intensely over and over again. The severity of their suffering is highlighted by the reference to the long furrows inflicted by the ploughmen (verse 3). This image recalls the sight of taskmasters whipping their slaves, causing long slash marks on the skin. This brings back memories of Egyptian enslavement, particularly the vulnerability of this nation that wasn't yet a nation (hence the reference to 'youth', verses 1–2). Of course it was an experience that was to be repeated in the life of Israel (especially in the exile), but because of such experience, Israel's faith in the Lord who 'cut me free' from oppression was deepened (verse 4).

171

## Praying ahead

Out of such memories comes hope. Out of such hope comes a
confident prayer that God's victory will be seen in the future too
through the demise of his enemies (verses 5–8). The prayer
concerns 'all who hate Zion', meaning everyone who rejects
what Zion stands for, that is, the Lord's presence and purposes
on earth. The desire is that all who fall in this category should
know the shame of defeat (verse 5), the despair of no provision
or future (verse 6), and the complete absence of blessing in their
lives (verse 8). This absence of blessing is expressed in a way
which indicates that real blessing is only to be found through
the presence and knowledge of the Lord. Hence this prayer is
based on the faith which has grown through the people's
experience, and it is the foundation of their confidence for all
that is to come in their lives.

## Questions

1. How do our prayers compare with this one? How far do we
   base our prayers on our experience of God?
2. What lessons have you learned about God through your life
   as an individual or as a church? How have you sensed his
   presence? And his absence ? How do these lessons influence
   our attitude to the future?
3. How might we help people who are going through hardships
   that seem totally unfair?

# With the Lord there is forgiveness and peace

---

**When we are deep in despair, our hope can be placed on the Lord alone. He will forgive us and restore us to quietness.**

---

### Confidence in God's mercy (Psalm 130)

Psalm 130 is one of seven penitential psalms which ask God for forgiveness based on sincere repentance (see also Psalms 6, 32, 38, 51, 102 and 143). As God's people we are always aware of our failure to live up to his perfect standards, and therefore we have to rely on God's mercy to sustain our relationship with him. This psalm expresses individual confidence in God's mercy, and this becomes the basis for a corporate confidence. The psalmist shows real boldness, because he is prepared to address God from the depths of his despair. He shows real faith, because he is able to affirm his belief in God's love and forgiveness despite his circumstances.

## Emerging from the depths

Despair and hope can live alongside each other. This psalm is about emerging from the pit of despair to find there's a rock of hope available (the theme is similar to that of Psalm 40). Compare the beginning and the end of the psalm. A transition takes place: the depths provide the opportunity for the heights of faith to be realized again.

The first four verses recognize that when despair is reached, there is no other place to turn than to God himself. But there is a problem. No-one can 'stand' before God (the implication of the rhetorical question in verse 3), because to 'stand' implies confidence, and sin bars the way to such a privileged position. Verse 4 gives the solution to the paradox: the forgiveness of God is greater than human failure! In other words, 'There's a way back to God from the dark paths of sin, there's a door that is open that you may go in'. The door is the forgiveness of God – his divine provision for sin. As verse 7 puts it, with the Lord there is 'full redemption', so sin can be the forerunner of salvation, not of condemnation. In turn salvation is the forerunner of restored relationship with God, marked by renewed reverence and awe as we live our lives in God's presence. This makes the end of verse 4 important. Forgiveness matters, not because it makes us feel better, but because it restores our relationship with God. The rest of the psalm is an exploration of what restored relationship with God means.

## Hoping in the Lord

The repeated theme of verses 5–8 is 'hope', and it is hope built upon faith that leads to the anticipation of salvation expressed in the words 'He [the Lord] himself will redeem Israel from all their sins' (verse 8). It is a certain hope, for it is compared with the watchman who longs for the morning, certain that it will come (verse 6). It is well-founded, because it emerges from the declared truth about God contained in his word (verse 5). This hope is therefore based on God's character, and his ability and desire to exercise his unfailing love and compassionate mercy.

This psalm presents us with the gospel in a nutshell! The good news is that Jesus was God's final answer to our need for forgiveness so that we might enjoy the relationship with God for which we are created. Jesus is the sure and certain hope which this psalm anticipates. Through him all sin is wonderfully dealt with and full redemption is provided. It is the truth which the writer of the Hebrews rejoices in throughout his letter. He encourages us 'since we have confidence to enter the Most Holy Place by the blood of Jesus . . . let us draw near to God with a sincere heart in full assurance of faith, having our hearts sprinkled to cleanse us . . . let us hold unswervingly to the hope we profess' (Hebrews 10:19–23).

## Simple trust (Psalm 131)

Psalm 131 has clear connections with the song of ascents which precedes it. It can be understood as the natural response to the overwhelming truth presented in Psalm 130: when we are confronted by the forgiveness of God, there is no option but to come humbly to the Lord in simple trust based in his sufficiency.

Verse 1 presents an attitude of grateful submission. Simple trust is not tainted by personal pride or ambition, but instead it adopts a humble position before the Lord. Verse 2 describes the calmness and tranquillity which comes from knowing that there is someone who can be relied on totally. The image of 'a weaned child' suggests dependence existing alongside a discovered independence. A weaned child has moved from being helpless to a position of security which still has childlike limitations.

The outcome is confidence and contentment in placing continued hope and trust in the person who has proved utterly trustworthy. This is the position of strength, not weakness, to which all God's people are called. When our hope is centred on the Lord we are truly aware of ourselves and our limits, as our focus becomes the unlimited nature of his merciful provision for us.

### Questions

1. What do we learn in Psalm 130 about forgiveness? Why is it needed? How is it obtained? What are its consequences?
2. Why do we ask for forgiveness from God or from others? How far are we driven primarily by self interest to feel better?
3. What 'depths' are you experiencing at the moment? Do you feel that you are emerging from them? How might you achieve this?

### The forgiveness of God

The different words which David uses in the psalms to describe his forgiveness are full of meaning.

In Psalm 51, for instance, the phrase 'blot out my transgressions' means to 'erase them so completely that no trace remains' (Exodus 32:32; Numbers 5:23; Colossians 2:14). The phrases 'Wash away all my iniquity and cleanse me from my sin' (verse 2) use a term applied to washing dirty clothing.

The three words he uses in Psalm 51:1–2 to describe his sin are also significant: 'transgression' ('to overstep the mark'), 'iniquity' ('to be morally corrupt') and 'sin' (which means 'missing the mark, failing to reach the divine standard and goal').

David also says he was 'sinful from the time my mother conceived me' (Psalm 51:5). J Oswald Sanders writes: 'David was not casting any reflection on his mother, or suggesting that conception is in itself sinful. Rather, he was indicating that he now saw that his outward crimes were only the expression of his inveterately sinful nature.'

When David says 'Cleanse me with hyssop' (Psalm 51:7), he is referring to the cleansing of a leper (someone suffering from some form of skin disease). Part of this process was to dip a bunch of hyssop in a container filled with blood and then to sprinkle it over the leper seven times (see Leviticus 14:6–7). Alternately, it could refer to the process of decontamination of a person who had been in contact with a dead body (Numbers 19:16–19).

# Psalm 132

## Promises, promises!

**We should honour the promises we make to the Lord.
The Lord honours the promises which he
makes to his people.**

This psalm is rather different from the other ascent songs. It is longer, uses other Old Testament passages, and is concerned with the outcome of promises made by David and the Lord himself. The first ten verses are based on David's promise to the Lord to find a resting place for the Ark (see 2 Samuel 6). Verses 8–10 are in parallel with the words of King Solomon on the occasion of the dedication of the temple (see 2 Chronicles 6:41–42).

The final eight verses recall the Lord's promise to David and his descendants (see 2 Samuel 7). The place of this psalm among the songs of ascents can be explained by the central place of Zion. The Lord and David both chose Zion as the special place of the Lord's presence (verse 13). The people in pilgrimage could rejoice in the Lord's presence and pray for his continued blessing upon Jerusalem with confidence that their will was at one with the will of their God.

### David's promise

We find it very difficult to honour some of our promises. Perhaps we make promises rashly, with no consideration of their effect on us or on other people. The promises which we make to God are the most difficult to keep, because they rely on our total commitment to God and his ways. David's commitment to his promise therefore provides us with a clear, if humbling, example.

David's promise caused him 'hardships' (verse 1), a term

177

which could refer to the opposition which he faced (including the Philistines). In making his promises David became so 'God-centred' that his personal needs and those of his family were given second place (verses 2–5). His commitment was unfailing. It was also made public so that the people who looked up to him were caught up with his vision (verses 6–7). They were prepared to move with the Ark to worship the Lord in the dwelling-place David would secure for him. The contrast between the personal hardship in verse 1 and the shared joy in verse 9 is stark. What a difference a carefully made promise (coupled with vision) can make.

## The Lord's promise

The promise of the Lord stands in parallel to that of David, and yet there are some important differences. First, David's promise is made unconditionally but is subject to human frailty, whereas the Lord's promise reflects his unfailing will which is established by his covenant love (verse 12). David's descendants will succeed him if they remember that their first loyalty is to the Lord (just as David's had been). Secondly, the Lord's promise has eternal effects ('for ever and ever' in verses 12 and 14). The Lord is not just *totally* committed but *permanently* committed to his promise.

The final two verses look forward to the coming Messiah, referring as they do to the Lord's 'anointed one' who will have a resplendent crown (a figure meaning royal glory and splendour). David too is described as 'anointed' (verse 10) and also as 'the lamp of Israel' (2 Samuel 21:17). In this way he prefigures the Messiah who is to come and who, in the Servant Songs of Isaiah, is also called 'servant'.

## Questions

1. What hardships have you suffered in your life because of your commitment to the Lord? How should we view such hardships? How did you get through them? Did the hardships ever turn to joy or blessing?
2. How much do you consider the consequences of promises

before you make them? What principles should be used to decide whether promises should be made or avoided?

3. What do we learn here about the character of the Lord and the nature of the promises he makes? How should this affect our lives as his people?

4. How does the ministry of Jesus reflect what this psalm leads us to expect?

## Anointing

To 'anoint' with oil was a common practice in biblical times (Ruth 3:3, 'perfume' NIV). It was a token of respect shown to a welcome guest, and failure to carry this out was seen as a lack of hospitality (Luke 7:46). People and things were anointed to signify that they were 'set apart' for a special God-given task. For example, Jacob anointed the stone he used as a 'pillow' on which to rest his head (Genesis 28:18). Prophets (1 Kings 19:16), priests (Leviticus 4:3) and kings (1 Samuel 10:1) were all anointed. David was anointed three times, first in anticipation of his kingship (1 Samuel 16:13), then as king over Judah (2 Samuel 2:4), then as king over all Israel (2 Samuel 5:3).

The phrase 'The LORD's anointed' was used to describe the king who was God's special choice (1 Samuel 12:3; Lamentations 4:20). The term 'anointed one', from which we get the word 'Messiah', is used in Psalm 132 to refer to David. Christians believe that this phrase ultimately refers to the Lord Jesus (see Daniel 9:25 and Acts 4:26). He combines within his own person the three anointed offices of Prophet, Priest and King.

## Covenant

The concept of covenant goes back to the book of Genesis (see Genesis 15:7–20). There God entered into a covenant with Abram, giving to him and his children territory which stretched from Egypt to the Euphrates. The Hebrew word is *Berith* meaning 'an agreement'. However, when it comes to a covenant between God and man we are not dealing with two equal parties. God's covenant is essentially a matter of grace (undeserved love, Psalm 89:28). His covenant is always linked with his 'covenant love' (*hesed*) or 'mercy' (see Genesis 9:15; Jeremiah 33:20–22). The word 'everlasting' or 'eternal' is used of God's covenant in various places (see Leviticus 24:8; Deuteronomy 33:9; Jeremiah 33:21; Malachi 2:4).

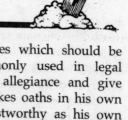

## Oaths

In the Bible oaths are solemn promises which should be undertaken carefully. They are commonly used in legal settlements and covenants to confirm allegiance and give assurance. It is noteworthy that God takes oaths in his own name because his promises are as trustworthy as his own faithful character (Hebrews 6:13–14). The Bible warns against thoughtless oath-making (see, e.g. Leviticus 5:4), an idea which completely contrasts to the nature of the oaths in Psalm 132:2, 11.

# Psalms 133–134

## It feels so good

---

**Meetings of the family of God are wonderful experiences because the Lord blesses his people by his presence.**

---

### Family unity (Psalm 133)

We all like to 'feel good' and that desire can affect what we wear, where we go, who we mix with, what we say and what we do. This psalm is written because of the 'feel good factor'. The pilgrims who meet together at Zion are like a united family as they are bonded to God and each other.

I expect we can all think of occasions in family life when the concord between family members has brought us real joy. Perhaps, like me, the face of a grandparent may come to mind as in their old age they look around their extended family with great pride and contentment. Or perhaps you can only wish that your family could be like this.

The good news is that when Christians meet together, we can sense a joy and unity which far surpasses anything we can know in human family relationships. The phrase 'brothers live together' was originally used to describe married brothers living in the same home (Deuteronomy 25:5), but throughout the Old and New Testament 'brother' describes God's people because their bonding to each other was 'brother-like' (or 'sister-like') in quality. Verse 1 rejoices in this wholesome experience: it is both good and thoroughly pleasant.

### As oil and dew

Such family unity is like 'oil' and 'dew' in at least three respects (verses 2–3a).

▶ These two images denote a *plentiful supply*. The oil is described as 'running down', suggesting a level of extravagance. The dew is identified as the dew from Mount Hermon which was probably a place known for an abundance of dew.

▶ They denote *refreshing provision*. Oil was used to refresh visitors upon their arrival, and dew refreshed the land.

▶ Both oil and dew serve to remind us of the *Lord's provision*. Oil was used to consecrate priests (Exodus 29:7; Leviticus 8:12) who served as God's mediators, and dew was always understood to be a sign of divine provision and blessing (see, for example, the way the image of dew is used in Hosea 14:4–5).

By using these two images the psalmist affirms that the experience of meeting together as God's people at Zion was one which exceeded expectations, was thoroughly refreshing, and an experience of grace from the Lord's hand.

The last sentence of verse 3 confirms that God chooses to bring blessing to his gathered people. In other words, it confirms that the wonderful 'feel good' experience is the result of God's grace and blessing; it is not human achievement, and it can last for ever. The final words also confirm that God chooses to give his blessing here to people together, not one by one. How we might miss out if we don't join in corporate acts of celebration like those the pilgrims held in Jerusalem! This corporate setting, plus the focus on the eternal quality of God's blessing, has led to the frequent use of this psalm at the Lord's Supper. This Christian gathering can bring refreshment beyond our expectations, and enables us to recognize more clearly the grace of our God in the provision of the Lord Jesus Christ as Saviour and Lord.

## Bless the Lord (Psalm 134)

This final song of ascents sums up people's reaction to the Zion pilgrimage: 'We've praised the Lord and he has blessed us' is their delighted response. This short song celebrates again the presence of God at Zion. This leads to the encouragement to praise the Lord, which is taken up in Psalms 135 and 136 ( so much so that Psalm 135 relies on Psalm 134 for its start and conclusion).

Some of our English translations use 'praise the Lord' instead of 'bless the Lord' to show that the phrase means to express our thanks and worship. When God is the object of blessing it means that he is pronounced holy and worthy of the joy and delight which our praise brings to him. The call to praise the Lord is addressed to those who 'minister by night in the house of the LORD' (verse 1), which may mean the Levites (in Deuteronomy 10:8 they are identified as those who minister before the Lord and pronounce blessings). The tasks of the Levites spanned night as well as day, for they administered both morning and evening sacrifices (see 1 Chronicles 9:33; 23:30). This would also make sense of 'lift up your hands' in verse 2, for we know that this was a gesture which accompanied Aaron's pronouncement of blessing (Leviticus 9:22). The use of raised hands in addressing the Lord in prayer appears often in the Psalms, both in pleading for mercy and in offering praise (see 28:2; 77:2; 63:4). It seems appropriate because it symbolizes both the desire to give to and receive from the Lord. Jesus himself raised his hands when he blessed his disciples following his resurrection (Luke 24:50).

### The Lord bless you

How many times have we said 'God bless' or 'may the Lord bless you' without any real consideration of the meaning and implication of this phrase? There is an awesome note in verse 3, for it recognizes that 'the LORD, the Maker of heaven and earth' is the source of the desired blessing. When people are blessed by the Lord, they may receive spiritual and material benefits in abundance. The other striking feature in verse 3 is the general nature of the blessing that is made. It identifies 'you' as the object of the Lord's blessing, and in so doing the experience of God's people throught their history is affirmed: where God's people find the presence of the Lord, there they also find blessing.

## Questions

1. What do you think would have been the attitude of the pilgrim people as they arrived in Jerusalem? Would this affect their experience? How far are we prepared to 'feel good'? Or do we fear the worst?

2. How does your experience of meeting with other members of God's family match up to the exuberance of this psalm? Why, or why not?

3. Do you find gestures helpful in worship? Which (remember that standing or kneeling is also a gesture, see below)?

4. Society seems to be falling apart all over the world so that everyone is more individualistic and consequently lonely. How can we reverse this state of affairs?

## Gestures in worship

Many different gestures and postures for worship are recorded in the Bible, and as non-verbal human communication they convey meaning. They particularly represent dependence before God and adoration. Scripture teaches that right attitudes are more important than right postures (e.g. Hebrews 12:28–29), but the latter can be a visible sign of appropriate heart attitudes, especially reverence and humility (see, e.g. Psalm 5:7). God's people are recorded as sitting (e.g. 2 Samuel 7:18), kneeling (e.g. Luke 22:41), standing (e.g. 1 Kings 8:22) and bowing down (e.g. Nehemiah 8:6) in praise and worship. More specifically, the raising of hands is recorded as a natural and meaningful gesture in prayer and praise (see, e.g. 1 Kings 8:54; Psalms 28:2; 63:4; 141:2).

# Psalm 135

## Why the hallelujahs?

**We must praise the Lord. His character demands it, creation declares it and history shows that he deserves it.**

'Why should I praise the Lord?' Have you ever asked yourself that question? Sometimes we think things aren't going very well for us so we feel like moaning at God rather than praising him. Other times we are all too aware of our failings and feel unworthy to praise the Lord. Frequently we just don't know where to start when it comes to praising other people, let alone God! Thankfully this psalm can help us out, in several ways.

- It reminds us that there is always something we can praise God for, because our own circumstance in the present is not the only reality we know. We can praise the Lord for the consistency of his nature and being. We can praise him for his creative power, and for past experiences of his goodness.

- It celebrates the Lord's compassion to his chosen people who, despite their failings, he always regards as his treasured possession.

- It's a psalm which we can always pick up and use whenever we feel unable to compose our own words of praise.

Psalm 135 uses words and phrases found in other Old Testament passages, including the two psalms which surround it and Psalm 115. Because of these connections it is sometimes described as a supplement to the Hallelujah Psalms or the songs of ascents.

## Praise the name of the Lord

The opening lines are an invitation to praise the Lord's name. His 'name' signifies all that he stands for, his nature and his will. It is, of course, the Lord's character which determines his will and purpose, and the first few verses focus on that. He is described as 'good' and 'great' (verses 3, 5), two characteristics which determine his purposes for he does 'whatever pleases him' (verse 6). His greatness is confirmed by his work in creation (verses 6–7), his success in setting his people free from oppression (verses 8–12), and his complete contrast with all other gods (verses 5, 15–18). However, his uniqueness of character and purpose can be fully appreciated only when his relationship with his chosen people is understood.

## Praise the Lord of the covenant

Although the word 'covenant' does not actually appear here, it is the uniting thread in this song of praise. God's choice makes Israel his precious people ('his treasured possession', verse 4). He intervened in the events of history for their sake and secured the promised land as their inheritance (verse 12; cf. Deuteronomy 6:1–3). Furthermore, the Lord worked for his people with justice and compassion (verse 14; cf. Exodus 34:6). Their hope is based upon his enduring reputation (verse 13). For these reasons the Lord's people are bold in their rejection of other gods (verses 15–18). They respond with undiluted praise as they are gathered in the city where his presence has been intimately experienced (verses 19–21).

## Questions

1. Can you recall any past events in your life when you have been struck by the greatness of the Lord? How did this make you feel?
2. What do we learn in this psalm about the Lord's relationship with his people? How can we show our gratitude to the Lord for his love for us?

3. Do you know anyone who adheres to another religious faith? How might this psalm affect your conversations together? Are you sometimes wary about tangling with them because they seem more able to debate than you do? What do you think would have happened to the confidence and faith of the people when they used this song for praise?
4. The final verses of Psalm 135 are all-inclusive. Do you really take part in worship at your church, or do you let it happen around you? Is praise a Christian duty?

# Psalm 136

## 'His love endures for ever'

**We are to give the Lord heartfelt and audible thanks because his limitless love is focused upon us for ever.**

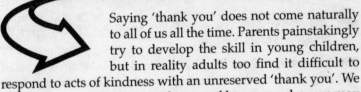

Saying 'thank you' does not come naturally to all of us all the time. Parents painstakingly try to develop the skill in young children, but in reality adults too find it difficult to respond to acts of kindness with an unreserved 'thank you'. We may feel too indebted, too embarrassed by our need, or we may simply forget, possibly because we take some acts of kindness for granted. The instruction in this psalm is not an option and it cannot be misunderstood: 'Give thanks' is repeated at its start and its end.

Psalm 136 is known as the 'great hallel', for it praises the Lord for his lasting love – the theme of the prominent refrain 'His love endures for ever'. This refrain declares the ultimate reason for the people's heartfelt thankfulness; the words are not idle ones, but commit the speakers to the faith which they express. In recalling the past outworking of God's love, this psalm is similar in design and theme to Psalm 135 with which there is some overlap.

## Thank you for your greatness

Verses 2, 3 and 26 suggest that the Lord is beyond all comparison and this is a reason to thank him. These verses contain superlatives: the Lord is 'God of gods', 'Lord of lords' and 'the God of heaven'. This means that:

▶ He is above all in terms of his *essential being* and because of his *immeasurable* power. Because he surpasses all else, he cannot be measured or compared with anyone or anything else.

▶ His every action on behalf of his people is therefore an act of his condescension and *grace*.

▶ He is also incomparable because his *love* does last *for ever*.

## Thank you for your wonders

Verse 4 introduces historical recollections in the remainder of the psalm by pointing out that the Lord 'alone does great wonders'. The word used for 'wonders' suggests works which are beyond our comprehension or understanding. The works recorded here were humanly speaking impossibilities:

▶ The whole creative activity of God is beyond comprehension (verses 5–9).

▶ The escape from Egypt and the demise of the Egyptian oppressors was an amazing chapter in the history of his people (verses 10–15).

▶ Their desert wanderings represented a whole catalogue of the Lord's marvellous interventions (verses 16–22).

It is the Lord's own greatness and grace which make the impossible possible. His wonders and miracles show us that his love does last for ever.

## Thank you for your provision

The experiences of God's love are summarized by three aspects of the Lord's provision for his people in verses 23–25.

▶ The Lord saw and acted for the lowest of nations (verse 23; cf. Deuteronomy 7:7–8).

▶ He brought freedom from those who desired his people's harm (verse 24).

▶ He provided the daily physical need of food (verse 25).

It is quite surprising that a section about wonders ends with a reference to the provision of what many of us take for granted, but for the Israelites their physical survival had depended upon the Lord's gift of food granted miraculously (manna and quail, Exodus 16). It was a symbol of their special place in the Lord's purposes. In all their needs they learned from the Lord that his love does last for ever.

So the psalm recalls the actions of the Lord's grace and expresses a faith which is built upon historical fact. Those who echo the words of its refrain appreciate the outworking of the Lord's grace in their life and recognize their dependence on him who is both capable and dependable.

## Questions

1. Do you believe in a God who can do miracles? Why don't we accredit wonders to God's hand very often? Do we put too much down to circumstances or good fortune? How might this affect our lives as Christians?

2. What does the 'incomparability' of the Lord mean to you? How does it affect your life and faith? Does he have rivals in our affairs? What are they?

3. Why is it fashionable to avoid mention of God by reference to 'the wisdom of Mother Nature', the 'Big Bang', 'Providence' and so on?

# Psalm 137

## How can we sing?

---

**We can overcome the pain of awful circumstances by persistent devotion and hope in the Lord.**

---

The opening words of this psalm are well known today as the title of the popular song by Boney M. However, the harsh vengeful words of the final verse are not quite so  popular or well-known, and this psalm needs to be understood as a whole. It laments the pain felt by God's people who had witnessed the fall of Jerusalem and the torment of the exile. The Babylonians had been responsible for the destruction of Jerusalem, and, along with their Edomite allies, had destroyed and looted the Israelite homeland. The memory of such events was painful and real. The people of God had wept (verse 1) and, had suffered torment (verse 3). They felt unable to sing their songs of faith because their circumstances appeared to deny the faith that these songs declared (verses 3–4). Their devotion was steadfast, however, for they found a song which could be sung – this psalm.

This song could be both composed and sung in the face of their tormentors because of their resilient faith. It is just as much a song of the Lord as any other of their psalms and religious songs. It expresses the resolve of this people and their unwavering devotion and trust in their Lord, while the eye of realism does not belittle the pain and despair which had governed the reality of Babylon. There is an obvious contrast in mood to Psalm 48 but the theology is the same: 'Great is the LORD, and most worthy of praise, in the city of our God, his holy mountain. It is beautiful in its loftiness, the joy of the whole earth … God is in her citadels; he has shown himself to be her fortress' (Psalm 48:1–3).

## We wept

The stark contrast between the start of this psalm and the psalms which precede it cannot be missed. Verse 2 uses the figure of hanging up harps to indicate that all rejoicing was, as it were, put on hold. The exile was an experience of isolation and alienation – the land was not their homeland, and enforced expulsion from homes gives rise to weeping – but also an experience of remembering. To some extent, remembering what Zion was like (see p. 163) and what it had become increased the pain (verse 1), but it also provided the reason for hope.

## We remembered

In verses 4–6 the writer commits himself to the task of remembering. The psalm itself was probably written after the exile experience had ended (hence the use of the past tense in the opening verses). The writer may well be writing upon his return to Jerusalem, now destroyed and desolate. Hence these verses remember the resolve that had been established in exile. Jerusalem was and is his 'highest joy' (verse 6). It was and is worth committing his life to – all he can do (represented by 'right hand') and say (represented by 'tongue') is worthless if Jerusalem is not his priority. It is through the establishing of this priority that the people's loyalty to the Lord is confirmed. They couldn't allow the Lord's songs to be misused as songs of entertainment for their tormentors (verse 3), nor could they use their songs while in a foreign (unclean) environment (verse 4). Their songs and their faith were tied up with their identity – something they must remember.

## We trust

The final three verses urge God himself to remember and not to forget. They really are a plea for justice. The people request that the Lord will balance the books and repay Edom and Babylon for the pleasure they took in Jerusalem's destruction. The people believe that, because the Babylonians have brought down the city of God, they are the ones whose fate is destruction (verse 8). It is impossible to miss the demand for the Lord to inflict painful revenge on Israel's oppressors – the figurative language in verse 9 is harsh, demanding severity of pain even to the most helpless. But the scandal of the revenge which is requested is matched by the humility of God's people as they entrust the matter into the hands of the God whose justice they depend upon.

## Questions

1. What does this psalm have to say about: (a) coping with difficult times; (b) belonging to God's people; and (c) attitudes to our enemies?
2. Should Christians ever pray for God's justice to fall on evil-doers? Why, or why not?
3. How does the weeping for Jerusalem in this psalm contrast with Jesus' weeping for Jerusalem (Luke 19:41–44)?
4. What comparisons can be made between the portrayal of Babylon and Jerusalem in this psalm and that which occurs in Revelation? (See, for example, Revelation 18 and 21.) What is the relevance for us today?

# Psalm 138

## All yours!

**All praise belongs to the Lord because our lives are a witness to his love and faithfulness.**

'I'm all yours'! What a relief this little sentence brings when we have been waiting for someone's attention. In this short psalm the singer sets his attention on the Lord: 'I'm all yours,' he says, 'I am available to you and have

responsibilities to you because of who you are and what you have done.' The psalm is created to bring praise to the Lord. As it follows Psalm 137 and has a number of themes common with the second part of Isaiah, it is usually considered to be an individual's praise for the return from exile. It obviously came to be used by the community at large as a suitable song to give the Lord thanks for his love and deliverance.

## I'm all yours

The psalm explores the implications of the writer's recognition that his whole life belongs to the Lord. First, he wants to praise the Lord with integrity and intensity (verses 1–2). This desire is emphasized by the variety of verbs which are used in these verses ('praise', 'sing', 'bow down'). The phrase 'before gods' could mean that the singer will be a witness to the Lord either before foreign gods or alongside heavenly beings who praise him. There is a sense of responsibility and a willingness to be counted as someone wholeheartedly committed to the Lord's worship.

The second implication of whole-life commitment to God is that every stage of life is in the Lord's hands. The writer refers to events which bear witness to the Lord's work of salvation, both past (verse 3) and present (verse 7), and this gives rise to the future hope expressed in the final verse. There is great confidence that it is the Lord who determines each path of life, and it is he who will perfect that life through the accomplishing of his purposes (verse 8). The future hope is one built on the faith accumulated through experience.

## The honour is all yours

This psalm is not an excuse for self-congratulation. The right to be praised belongs to the Lord, and the honour and glory are his by divine right. In other psalms human beings exalt the Lord, but here the point is made that it is the Lord who exalts his name and his word (verse 2). The phrase actually means that the Lord has exalted his 'word above his name', perhaps indicating that the Lord's promises of salvation have been given the place of highest honour among everything that his name stands for. The Lord's honour is even recognizable by kings who will see the Lord's great glory (verses 4–5).

Verse 6 brings a qualification to this idea of glory: the Lord's glory is seen through his concern for those who are 'lowly'. His glory is one which reaches down, not one which makes reaching up necessary. The fact is that those who try to exalt themselves will never really witness the Lord's glory and will always be far away from him. The psalmist's own experience of trouble serves to bring the psalm to its climax. It is all about the Lord's hand of salvation (verse 7). It is this above all which brings him glory. It is this which makes his love an unrivalled enduring quality for the sake of every work of his hand (verse 8). In this final reference the universal perspective is regained: all honour is the Lord's, all creation belongs to him.

## Questions

1. The second half of verse 3 suggests that the writer was changed through his prayer. Do we always ask for circumstances to change while we stay the same? How might God answer your prayers by changing you? Why do we sometimes change our views and perspectives when we pray?
2. What might it mean to praise God 'half-heartedly'? What can we do to ensure whole-hearted praise? (This psalm says something about variety in praise, posture, location, attitude, as well as subject matter!)
3. Why is the world in general so hostile to Christianity?

# Psalm 139

## The Lord knows me inside out

---

**We can never fool the Lord for he knows everything about us.**

---

It can be rather scary when we think that friends know us so well that we can't hide anything from them. We may feel a bit transparent or vulnerable. On the whole, though, we are probably grateful because a friend who knows us 'inside out' has accepted us for who we really are, and we have no need to be anything other than ourselves. What a lot of pressure that relieves us from! It also means that our friend is able to give us appropriate advice and support, and is able to trust us even if other people neglect or misunderstand us. This psalm celebrates the fact that God himself knows us through and through. The psalmist is relieved and happy to know that no part of his personality or life is hidden from the penetrating eyes of God. This gives the psalmist a sense of joy, wonder and comfort – the pressure valve is released.

This is the beginning of a set of psalms (Psalms 139–145) which are associated with David. Each explores the knowledge and nearness of God to his people in the context of heartfelt adoration. The climax to these themes is reached in Psalm 145.

### You know me

The first four verses confirm the psalmist's belief that God knows all there is to know about him. He addresses God as 'O LORD', to express adoration of him as the all-knowing one. But these four verses, along with verses 23–24, also indicate that the psalmist considers God to be his judge; the Lord is the one who searches and discerns, perceives and tests. It seems likely, because of the content of verses 19–22, that the psalmist was aware of enemies who opposed him and God. He is confident that the Lord will acquit the innocent and punish the guilty, because no-one can escape the Lord's presence. This is the basis of his reflection and the cause of his wonder.

## You are near me

Sometimes verses 7–12 have been understood to mean that the psalmist was longing to 'flee' from God's presence. But this does not seem to fit with the rest of the psalm. Instead, these verses humbly and gratefully recognize that the Lord is everywhere, including the psalmist's very body itself. The Lord surrounds his servant and 'hems' him in. This is not an image of restricting movement and activity but conveys protection; the Lord's hand is upon him to protect, to guide and to hold him secure (verses 5, 10), everywhere (verses 7–10) and at all times (verses 11–12).

## You created me

Verses 13–16 are the core of the psalm. God's knowledge and judgment is related to his role as creator. The psalmist acknowledges God as his creator, not just a work in the past but an ongoing work covering the whole of his life. The Lord creates the 'inner me' ('my inmost being', verse 13) and the 'outer me' ('my frame', verse 15). His work of creation began in the womb (verse 13), concerned the whole of life and even determined how long the psalmist would live (verse 16). In the light of all this, the words of verse 14 are pure and confident adoration. There is wonder and reverent fear, but this is fear which builds you up and results in praise, it does not crush or condemn.

## You are beyond me

'How precious ... how vast' is the only way the psalmist can sum up his certain yet mind-blowing understanding of the Lord's creative care and all-knowing presence. Just a partial glimpse of God is too much for the human mind to take in. The psalmist can only recognize that he is overwhelmed and out of his depth, and he expresses his confidence that his life is lived with God (verses 17–18). In fact the little phrase 'when I awake' may indicate that the psalmist is confident that even beyond this life he will awake in the Lord's presence.

### So I'm for ever grateful

The psalm ends with two expressions of gratitude. First the psalmist commits himself to the Lord (verses 19–22): he is saying, 'I am on the Lord's side. I set myself against those who set themselves against the Lord.' This commitment is an active form of gratitude. The psalmist has caught a glimpse of who God is, and he responds in a way which affects his life.

Secondly, the psalmist expresses his gratitude by laying himself open to the Lord again, saying in effect: 'Be my judge, put me right and lead me in your way for ever' (verses 23–24). The way in which the opening verses are reflected in these last two verses gives urgency to his request: seeing the Lord as he is, if only in part, leads to a desire to be right with him and at one with him.

### Questions

1. How does the fact that God knows you inside and out make you feel? Why do you feel this way?
2. Why are verses 13–16 significant when we consider issues like abortion, suicide and euthanasia?
3. What demands do verses 5–12 make on our lives?
4. How can an atheist be sure that there is no God when he or she thinks about the wonders of DNA and the vastness of the universe?

### The hand of God

The hand of God symbolizes his redemptive and creative power (Isaiah 49:2; 62:3) and the protection and strength which he gives to his people (Ezra 8:31; Psalm 110:5). The hand of God is the instrument of his blessing (Ezra 7:6) and provision (Psalm 145:16) and it fulfils God's purposes (Acts 11:21). In this psalm the Lord's 'hand' is mentioned in verses 5 and 10 to stress his absolute control in human life. When the Lord's 'right hand' is specified, it usually serves to emphasize that the Lord is able to save (Psalm 138:7), for he gives help like a defence witness who stands to the right of the person being defended (Psalms 16:8; 109:31; 121:5; Isaiah 41:13). The place at the right hand of God is a position of honour and authority which Jesus occupies (Acts 7:55–56; Romans 8:34; Hebrews 1:3).

# Psalm 140

## Protect me, Lord

**The Lord acts as our deliverer, even when we face the most extreme and malicious schemes of wicked people.**

We don't very often face the sort of violence and evil which led to the composition of this psalm. Perhaps David endured this experience in the course of military battle (see verses 2 and 7). What is clear is that this psalm is about coming to the end of human resources of strength. It's about calling to God with confidence that he will come to our aid. Its theme is taken from the preceding psalm, for the prayer here is that the Lord will show that he is on the side of the righteous, just as the psalmist declared he is on the Lord's side (Psalm 139:19–22).

David makes this prayer because he is aware of the schemes of the wicked, the reality of his own need and the character of the Lord.

Wicked people are identified as those who promote 'violence (verse 1), make 'evil plans' (verse 2) and 'stir up war' (verse 2).

Their speech is like poison (verse 3), they are 'proud' and have 'set traps' (verse 5). All these activities show their commitment to bring about the downfall of the psalmist. Faced with this intensive campaign of hate, David prays for two things: personal protection ('rescue', 'protect', 'keep', verses 1–4), and the undoing of the unrighteous (their desires, plans, aspirations and future, verses 7–11).

The psalmist is certain of his own allegiance to God, and he has the confidence to align himself with the needy and the righteous for whom God secures justice (verses 12–13). The legal terms used ('the cause of the needy') suggest that he is aware that God is his advocate. He regards himself as one of the righteous, and his responsibility is to praise the Lord and live his life appropriately in the Lord's presence. Personal allegiance to the Lord is the basis on which his cry to the Lord is made.

The core of this psalm is 'You are my God' (verse 6). The successive use of the first person pronouns underlines David's commitment which underpins this prayer. It is a prayer that God will show his allegiance to his servant. He is 'Yahweh', 'the LORD' – Lord of the covenant – who hears the cry of his people because he is attentive to them. What's more, he is a strong saviour, who is willing and able to protect his people, not least through his opposition to those who threaten their well-being (verses 6–8).

Rather than just being an urgent plea for the Lord's help, this psalm is an expression of covenant faith and loyalty, without which this prayer could find no justification. It is based in the fundamental call to faith which God's people always must remember: 'what does the LORD your God ask of you but to fear the LORD your God, to walk in all his ways, to love him, to serve the LORD your God with all your heart and with all your soul ... He defends the cause of the fatherless and the widow ... He is your praise; he is your God' (Deuteronomy 10:12–22).

## Questions

1. Verse 3 of this psalm is used in Romans 3:13. How is the picture used there? What does this suggest about Paul's understanding of the psalm?

2. Do situations in which you find yourself alter what you feel about your faith? What do we learn from this psalm about consistent faith? What is its basis? How can it be expressed?
3. How far is the world hostile to Christianity or merely indifferent? Which is easier for us to cope with?

# Psalm 141

## Mixed company

**We need to pray that we will be drawn to what is good and not to what is evil.**

Life is lived in mixed company. Wherever we go we meet different people with different views, principles and ideologies. This psalm recognizes that there is a danger here: we may compromise our allegiance to God. The urgent request is that evil will be overthrown and defeated as the Lord intervenes in response to this prayer. The words 'Let not my heart be drawn to what is evil' (verse 4) are reminiscent of the familiar words of the Lord's prayer 'lead us not into temptation' (Matthew 6:13; Luke 11:4). We would do well to remember the portrayal of temptation in this psalm when we say the Lord's prayer, for the implications of its meaning should not be belittled.

## Not taking part ...

The first two verses reveal a sense of urgency and importance. The psalmist knows it is important that the Lord receives his prayer speedily. He is reliant on the Lord's help in terms of guarding his mind, will and words. The Lord's knowledge of all our ways has been acknowledged in the preceding psalms, but now David requests that the Lord might anticipate our tendency to be drawn to what is evil, to prevent us from taking part in wicked words, thoughts and deeds (verses 3–4). The final phrase of verse 4 probably refers to enjoying spending time (e.g. over meals) with wicked people, and may reflect proverbial statements like those found in Proverbs 12:26 and 22:24–25 (see also Jeremiah 9:4–6; 1 Corinthians 15:33; James 4:4). The psalmist wants no part in the ways of wicked people and declares that his prayer is set against them (verse 5b). He prays for their end and his own justification (verses 6–7).

### ... But being set apart

Once more the psalmist confirms that he is standing with the Lord. He is in a separate category: he cannot be confused with wicked people because the Lord is his goal, the focus of his life (verse 8). There are two consequences: first, he enjoys the company, help and advice of other God-centred people (verse 5; cf. Proverbs 27:6 and Psalm 140:13); and secondly, he is set apart for safety (verse 10). This final verse gives expression to confidence and faith. All life's snares and entrapments are of no significance when we are set apart in God our refuge: 'O sovereign LORD, in you I take refuge' (verse 8).

### Questions

1. Is it really important to 'keep good company'? How can we do this when our loyalties to family and our work situations bring us into contact with so many people who reject God's claim on their lives?
2. What particular temptations are we susceptible to? What are we 'drawn to'? Does it concern our use of words, the places we go, the TV we watch, the things we read, our use of imagination? Do we really choose to be 'set apart for the Lord'?

# Psalm 142

## Who cares?

---

**When it seems that nobody cares, remember that the Lord has committed himself to care for us.**

---

There's nothing quite so isolating as the belief that nobody cares for us. It makes us feel unwanted and undervalued, depressed and without hope for the future. We feel like  giving up and throwing in the hat. Such feelings are those which the psalmist identifies as his state of 'desperate need' (verse 6). He feels neglected and rejected and yet, as he poses the question 'who cares?', he is certain that the Lord does care for him. The result is this short prayer, in which despair is relieved by expressing trust in the Lord's goodness.

The title of this psalm links it with Psalm 57, which is also assigned to David's experience in the cave. Whereas Psalm 57 is full of confidence, Psalm 142 is a personal struggle to gain confidence when dire circumstances overwhelm David and threaten his faith. In content Psalm 142 is a new expression of the themes which we have met already in Psalms 140 and 141.

### Lord, you care

In despair the psalmist can do nothing else but turn to the Lord. There is a sense of urgency and openness as the one who feels so weak and entrapped (verse 3) repeats that his cry is a desperate entreaty to the Lord (verses 1–2, 5–6). The psalmist says that the Lord is all he needs and wants (his 'refuge' and 'portion', verse 5). This declaration is a recognition of the Lord's care, and it hints at the faith which inspires this plea for help. With eyes now turned to the Lord, the concluding expression of hope in verse 7 can be made: the Lord can bring release from trouble and he will be praised for his undisputed goodness and care. In the course of this prayer, personal and present despair gives way to shared and future hope.

## Questions

1. Why does God require us to pray to him? How does the psalmist grow in faith as he prays?
2. What can we do to encourage people who feel nobody cares about them? What people feel like that today? Why do they feel like that?

## Portion

A 'portion' originally referred to a proportion of land allotted when the land was divided for the tribes' inheritance (Numbers 26:52–56). In Deuteronomy 10:9 it is stated that the tribe of Levi was not allotted land because their portion was the Lord. This may indicate that the tribe's livelihood was to be derived from their administration of sacrifices, but it also seems to suggest that the Levites had a special relationship with the Lord. By claiming that the Lord is his portion (Psalm 142:5), the psalmist is recognizing that his life and livelihood are dependent on God's provision and grace (see also Psalms 16:5; 73:26; 119:57). What God provides for him and means to him is the basis of his inheritance.

# Psalm 143

## Help me, I'm preoccupied!

---

**We can be preoccupied with personal sin or circumstances, but only the Lord can bring real help and consolation.**

This psalm is the last of the seven 'penitential psalms' (see Psalm 130). Verses 1 and 2 reflect the theme of repentance and the hope for deliverance, but awareness of guilt is only one of the psalmist's preoccupations. He is especially aware of his human enemies (verses 3, 9, 12). Here again is a mixture of despair and faith, because personal sinfulness and the threatening environment lead to dependency upon the Lord. In many ways the psalm is a journey of faith discovery. Preoccupation with the difficulties of human life and experience fade into insignificance when confronted with the Lord whose past activity provides the reason for renewed hope. We all do well to take a fresh look at what takes up our attention: is it our weaknesses and difficulties, or is it the Lord's ability to deliver us from our failings and concerns?

### Lord, I turn to you

David pleads for the Lord's attention because he is in need of mercy (verse 1). This cry for mercy depends on the Lord's faithfulness and righteousness. These two characteristics underpin the covenant relationship with which the psalmist aligns himself when he calls himself the Lord's 'servant' (verse 2). David is aware of his own sinfulness as a human being, and this brings human nature and divine nature into stark contrast with each other. It is this realization which encourages him to cry for mercy, for the Lord is implored not to condemn but to bring 'relief' (verses 1 and 2). Relief from judgment and oppression is needed. Oppression comes in the form of an enemy who pursues the psalmist with so much vigour that he is crushed and life becomes like death (verses 3–4). There is no doubt that preoccupation with personal sin and external oppression brings real despair. That despair leads the psalmist to look back to discover a source of hope in order to look forward once again.

### Lord, I long for you

Verses 5 and 6 express a longing for the Lord to act as he has done in the past. It is an appeal based on the history of God's dealings with his people, for this illustrates the Lord's covenant commitment to them. Their history tells the story of a God who is active among his people and, by spreading out his hands, the psalmist shows that he is open to God's work and is in desperate need of God all over again.

### Lord, I trust you

The next section of the psalm (verses 7–10) expresses renewed confidence. The original plea is widened as the implications of God's merciful nature and activity are explored. The confidence is explained in a nutshell in verse 8: it is based on the Lord's 'unfailing love' (covenant love), and on the trust which that love evokes and sustains. It restates the discovery expressed in Psalm 37:5, that committing our way to the Lord means trusting him to work. Verses 7–10 present a whole series of requests which are inspired by this trust:

- 'Answer me quickly . . .' (verse 7a).
- Show me yourself ('Do not hide your face . . .', 'Bring me word . . .') (verses 7b, 8a).
- Guide me ('show me the way . . .', 'lead me . .') (verses 8b, 10b).
- 'Rescue me . . .' (verse 9).
- 'Teach me . . .' (verse 10).

These requests reflect the psalmist's sense of weakness: he knows he needs quick intervention. But his requests also express his commitment to stay close to the Lord in the future. There is a desire to live a God-directed life (verses 8, 10). It is only a Spirit-led life that is as free from difficulties as walking on level ground.

## Lord, I serve you

The declaration 'I am your servant' (verse 12) reminds us of the earlier words of verse 2, and it confirms that relationship to the Lord is the basis of the prayers contained in this psalm. David has no personal merit besides that which is derived from his relationship with the Lord. Once more it is the Lord's righteousness and love which mean that his deliverance is dependable (verses 11–12). At the start of the psalm it is despair which preoccupies the psalmist; at its end it is the Lord himself.

## Questions

1. How would you define penitence or repentance? How does your definition tie up with the content of this psalm?
2. Can you explain the meaning of verse 2? (Romans 3:20 and Galatians 2:16 might help.) How do you understand the work of Christ in this regard?
3. Do we as individuals and churches really desire to do God's will? Or are we only concerned with being saved from crisis? How did Jesus' commitment to the Father's will influence his prayers and his life? How do our priorities influence our prayers and our lives?

# Psalms 144–145

## Amazing grace

---

**We are insignificant when compared with the Lord's might and power, but the Lord is gracious towards us, and we need to declare his praise.**

### I praise the Lord, my rock (Psalm 144)

Psalm 144 celebrates God's grace and goodness. It draws its content from other psalms almost entirely, especially Psalm 18, but there are also parallels with Psalms 8, 33 and, to a lesser extent, 39, 102, 109, 127 and 128. Much of the psalm's content has therefore been commented on elsewhere, but it is still worth asking what this particular composition says to us. In terms of mood, there is both confidence and reflection. The interplay between these themes suggests that the person who compiled Psalm 144 was moved to reflection, awe and mystery through his confident declarations concerning the Lord's work in his life. For example, verses 1 and 2 lead to the reflection in verses 3 and 4. The psalm is associated with David, although its compiler may have been a leader who recalled words of David to remind the community of their heritage as God's people. Note that the singular pronouns (verses 1–11) become plural pronouns (verses 12–15) as the application of the psalm's message reaches beyond the individual to all people who name the Lord as their God (verse 15). The psalmist realizes that it is amazing that the Lord who is beyond us and over us is also with us and for us. This is grace in action, demonstrating covenant relationship with the Lord.

The first eleven verses describe the Lord's action on behalf of his chosen servant. The Lord is the rock and deliverer who provides his servant with the training, love and protection he needs (verses 1–2). The psalmist recognizes that he does not deserve this (verses 3–4, cf. Psalms 8:4; 18:3–4, 31, 34). The power and might of the Lord are emphasized by the descriptions of the Lord's activity in verses 5–8 (cf. Psalm 18:7–12). This leads to the psalmist restating his intention to bring praise to the Lord in verses 9 and 10 (cf. Psalms 18:49–50; 33:2), followed by a renewed cry for help (verse 11). So this first part of the psalm is saying 'The Lord is the rock and I don't deserve it. He is mighty to deliver and I need that deliverance again.'

Verses 12–15 celebrate what it means to receive God's grace. The message is that those who are the Lord's people know blessing in family life and experience prosperity and security (see also Psalms 127:3–5; 128:3). Verse 15 makes it abundantly clear that the psalm is not merely a celebration of deliverance and blessing. Rather, it is a celebration of what it means to be people under grace. This is after all what belonging to 'the people of the Lord' is all about.

## Make known the Lord's greatness (Psalm 145)

Confession of faith and an evangelistic message come together in Psalm 145, which serves both as a conclusion to the psalms of David which precede it and as an introduction to the Hallelujah Psalms which follow it. The psalm's content makes praise imperative, both as a means of confirming and propagating faith. The language of this acrostic psalm (each sentence begins with a successive letter of the Hebrew alphabet) is borrowed from elsewhere in the Psalter – making use particularly of Psalms 103, 104 and 111. Like Psalm 144 it recalls well-known statements about God and his work and places them in a fresh framework. The use of the acrostic structure seems appropriate because it was often used to aid the memory of essential truths of faith and belief. The psalm has been used over the centuries as the basis for many Christian songs, and it appears in a variety of liturgical readings. In theme and mood it is similar to the inspired song of Mary (Luke 1:52–53).

### I praise the Lord

The first ten verses express a personal commitment to praise the Lord, based upon one of the earliest confessions of God's loyalty to his people. Verses 8 and 9 make use of Exodus 34:6, a passage that is helpfully described as an early creed because it expresses the heart of Israelite belief about who God is and what he is like to his people. The crescendo of praise in these verses reaches its summit with this confession: praise and worship is the only response of creation to the creator who is mighty and majestic yet gracious and compassionate. The focus is awesome and universal and yet intimate and personal.

### The Lord is king

In theme Psalm 145 has much in common with those which describe the Lord as the universal king. This idea is there at the start as the psalmist owns the Lord as 'my God the King' (verse 1), and it is there at the psalm's centre in verses 11–13. God's glory will be told out so that through the witness of his people 'all people may know' how splendid is the glory of the Lord (verses 10–12). The manifestation of the Lord's glory is linked with a responsibility to praise him. To those whom the Lord has called by his gracious compassion, there is no such thing as worship without witness.

### Let everything that has breath praise the Lord!

As king, the Lord governs by providing for the needs of his people (verses 14–20). The scope is universal, for God provides for 'all he has made' (verse 13) and this point is emphasized by the repeated use of 'all'. He raises the spirits of discouraged people (verse 14), and gives food and provision (verses 15–16). He answers, watches over and saves those who follow his ways (verses 18–20). But the real miracle is that all this is established for ever because it is dependent on who God is and he is in essence loving to 'all he has made' (verses 8–9, 13, 17). In this psalm personal praise joins with the corporate praise of all creation (verse 21), praise which inspires devotion and worship, service and witness.

### Questions

1. Write a psalm of your own in celebration of your status

among the people of God. Remember to include thanksgiving for demonstrations of God's grace in your experience, both as an individual and as a member of the community of God's people locally and worldwide.

2. What can we do to make known God's glory in our society, our world? What should be at the heart of our message?

3. Does this psalm agree with the view that witness is a form of worship and worship a form of witness? Can you do both at once in, for instance, a Good Friday procession to your church; an open-air Remembrance Day Service; a March for Jesus? Does our view make any difference to our lives?

# Psalms 146–150: Note

These final five psalms unite to extol the praiseworthiness of the Lord. Each begins and ends with the words 'Praise the LORD' ('Hallelujah') and they have themes in common with the earlier group of Hallelujah Psalms (Psalms 111–113). They conclude Book 5 of the Psalms and the Psalter as a whole, so the journey of faith has moved from a focus on the law of God (Psalm 1) to an appreciation of the Lord's gracious love for his people borne out by the experiences of life. The paradox of divine greatness and compassion coming together results in unhindered and liberating praise which all creation enjoys and shares together for ever.

# Psalms 146–147

## The Lord helps and blesses us

**Put your trust in the Creator God, not in anything he has created.**

### The Lord reigns to help us (Psalm 146)

The sentiments of Psalm 146 have been expressed in one way or another in other psalms. The Lord reigns in a way which is in complete contrast with any human rule. The reigns of earthly kings have been appreciated elsewhere in the Psalter – usually in terms of God's provision for his people – but the Lord's rule surpasses any other. The Lord alone is totally trustworthy, for his rule does not come to an end (verses 3–4, 10). He is after all the creator who remains faithful for ever (verses 5–6) providing for his people's physical, emotional and spiritual needs, even when other people overlook or oppress them (verses 7–9). He is the God of the living for ever, and therefore his praise will resound as long as life remains (verse 2). The psalm affirms that the Lord reigns to help us and we live to praise him.

### The Lord acts to bless us (Psalm 147)

Psalm 147 has at its centre the activity of God. What God is and what he does stand together, even if there is something bewildering and overwhelming about the way this is achieved. It is the greatness of God which enables him to intervene for the needy, for he uses his power for our good (verses 1–11). The first eleven verses present various signs of the Lord's blessing, bringing to mind the phrase which was first used in Psalm 2, 'Blessed are all who take refuge in him' (Psalm 2:12). The result of such trust is security and peace which verses 12–14 celebrate

– in common with Psalm 125 (and the following songs of ascents).

Both the songs of ascents and this psalm give emphasis to the special place Israel has as recipient of the Lord's blessing. In verses 15–20 blessing is the revealed word of the Lord. Its movement is quick and unstoppable, for it is at the disposal of the Lord of all – just as creation itself is. The point is that the word of the Lord gives direction ('command', verse 15) and nothing can hinder its communication. Praise is therefore both fitting and pleasurable, for it is further communication between the Lord and his people.

## Questions

1. In what ways is God like, or unlike, a human king? Does it help to describe him as our king?
2. 'Make music to our God on the harp' (Psalm 147:7). What advantages are there in having an organ, a piano, guitars, a music group and choir? Should we try to please everyone in our church? If not, whom should we please? What is important to God?

# Psalms 148–150

## . . . so praise the Lord, everybody!

---

**Take a deep breath and use it in praise to the Lord.**

---

### All creation, praise the Lord!
### (Psalm 148)

This psalm calls the whole of creation to give the Lord the praise he deserves and which they owe to him. The all-inclusive nature of the call to praise is emphasized by the division of the universe into heaven (verses 1–6) and earth (verses 7–12). The final two verses of the psalm prepare for the more focused call to praise in Psalm 149, which concentrates on the praise which God's people themselves owe to him. God's people are part of the choir of the universe – but an important part. Just as the praise of heaven is seen in the praise of the earth, the praise of the earth is seen in the praise of his people. Three reasons for praise are given:

▶ The Lord created and established the heavens for ever (verses 5–6).

▶ The Lord is exalted above heaven and earth (verse 13).

▶ The Lord has given his people 'a horn' (verse 14).

The word 'horn' symbolizes strength and here appears to allude to a strong king who will bring honour to his people. Praising God brings honour and glory too, because through it God's people are recognized as those 'close to his heart' (verse 14). This is an astounding phrase; in the context of all the universe, God's people occupy the place close to his heart. It means that his people are uniquely valued and intimately precious to him. This, of course, while astounding, is the foundational principle of covenant faith and Christian belief: the Lord has set his love

213

on us (Deuteronomy 7:7) – so, indeed, what other nation has its gods near them 'the way the LORD our God is near us' (Deuteronomy 4:7)? We are close to God's heart and he is therefore close to us. This is the reason for resounding and jubilant praise.

## All Israel, praise the Lord! (Psalm 149)

Psalm 149 couples the task of praise with that of upholding justice. Both tasks are assigned to God's people and both will lead to the glory of God's people. The term 'saints' punctuates the psalm (verses 1, 5, 9) and really means the ones who are faithful among the worshipping community. It is the faithful and dedicated people of God who are to be involved with praise and justice, for they share in the work and therefore the glory of God. In other words, giving praise and administering justice are related to being close to the heart of God. They are tasks which depend on him and glorify him. Verse 6 is pivotal, for it emphasizes that praising the Lord will always be accompanied by practical involvement and action within the context of human affairs. The joy of praise (verses 2–5) clearly contrasts with the pain of inflicting punishment (verses 6–9). However, there is no conflict, because the glory of Israel is found in participating in the work of the Lord in whom there is holy unity. His name is to be praised!

## Praise the Lord with all you've got! (Psalm 150)

Book five of the Psalms comes to an end with a psalm wholly devoted to praise. Over the years this psalm has been given a variety of grand and poetic titles which, while recognizing its literary qualities, may undermine its essential message. This message is really about leaving behind the dignity of conventional restraints and discovering enthusiastic freedom in the praise of the Lord. The pace of the psalm demands the responses of 'everything that has breath' (verse 6), for every such creature owns life which is bound up with the Lord's 'acts of power' and 'his surpassing greatness' (verse 2). 'Praise him any way you like' is the psalm's message. Praise is about self-abandonment in energy and enthusiasm which is directed to God alone. It means making use of all your bodily functions – blow, pluck, bang and dance the Lord's praise! It means making use of every possible instrument and energy at your disposal – including your very breath. The psalm's simple yet challenging instruction is to praise the Lord any way you like, as long as you really praise him with all you've got.

These last five psalms instruct us to 'Praise the LORD'! The Lord commands it and desires it, we owe it and delight in it. Praise is his glory and our glory and through it we enjoy him for ever.

## Questions

1. Do we really believe that praise and involvement in social justice stand or fall together as Psalm 149 suggests? What do we need to do to fulfil the responsibilities which this psalm places on God's people? How might our lives be re-ordered? Do we support Christian organizations which have social concern at their heart?

2. A recent Christian song speaks of becoming 'even more undignified' in the praise and worship of God. What do you think about this? Do you think we should be prepared to be 'undignified' in praise? What does it mean? What are the dangers or advantages of seeing praise as an abandonment of self?

3. Whether you are feeling oppressed or uncared for today or not, re-read these last five psalms. Dwell on the fact that God's people are close to his heart, and that he upholds your cause and sustains you. What's more, your praise is important to the Lord in heaven and earth. So praise him with all you've got!

*Praise God, from whom all blessings flow,*
*Praise him, all creatures here below,*
*Praise him, above you heavenly hosts,*
*Praise Father, Son and Holy Ghost.*

# Further reading

John Goldingay, *Songs from a Strange Land: Psalms 42–51* (IVP, 1978).

Derek Kidner, *Psalms 1–72* (Tyndale Old Testament Commentary; IVP, 1973), *Psalms 73–150* (IVP, 1975).

G. A. F. Knight, *Psalms*, vols. 1 and 2 (The Daily Study Bible; St Andrew's Press, 1983).

C. S. Lewis, *Reflections on the Psalms* (Fontana/Collins, 1961).

Tremper Longman II, *How to Read the Psalms* (IVP, 1988).

C. H. Spurgeon, *Psalms*, vols. 1 and 2 (Crossway Classic Commentary; Crossway Books, 1993).

C. H. Spurgeon, *The Treasury of David*, vols. 1–7 (Evangelical Press, 1977).

John Stott, *Favourite Psalms* (Candle Books, 1994).